D0170540

HOW DO YOU GO TO THE
BATHROOM IN SPACE?

AC14069

0 1191 0099724 4

629.45
POG

HOW DO YOU GO TO THE BATHROOM IN SPACE?

Revised Edition

William R. Pogue, Astronaut

Introduction by
John Glenn

Cartoons by Sidney Harris

TOR®

A Tom Doherty Associates Book
New York

BLUE RIDGE LIBRARY
28 AVERY ROW
ROANOKE, VIRGINIA 24012-8828

HOW DO YOU GO TO THE BATHROOM IN SPACE?

Copyright © 1999 by William R. Pogue

All rights reserved, including the right to reproduce this book,
or portions thereof, in any form.

This book is printed on acid-free paper.

Cartoons by Sidney Harris
Photographs courtesy of NASA

A Tor Book
Published by Tom Doherty Associates, LLC
175 Fifth Avenue
New York, NY 10010

www.tor.com

Tor® is a registered trademark of Tom Doherty Associates, LLC.

Library of Congress Cataloging-in-Publication Data

Pogue, William R.
   How do you go to the bathroom in space? / William R. Pogue;
cartoons by Sidney Harris.—2nd ed.
      p.   cm.
   Includes bibliographical references and index.
   ISBN 0–312–87295–X
   1. Astronautics Miscellanea.   2. Pogue, William R. Anecdotes.
I. Title.
TL793.P54 1999
629.45—dc21   99–36192

Revised Edition: October 1999

Printed in the United States of America

0   9   8   7   6   5   4   3   2   1

ACKNOWLEDGMENTS

I received considerable assistance during the second revision of this book. The Office of Public Affairs at the Johnson Space Center was especially helpful in providing current technical information on new programs related to the Shuttle and the International Space Station. Mike Gentry at Johnson was a great help in locating photographs and illustrations. I also received substantial encouragement and suggestions from the staff that administers the NASA Aerospace Education Services Project at Oklahoma State University. I wish to thank the many people who have posed new questions by postal mail and E-mail.

I am grateful to my agent and good friend, Barbara Bova, who deserves the credit for getting the original book published and who continues to support the effort with her enthusiasm and professional skills. At Tor Books, thanks go to Kathleen Doherty for launching the revision and providing up-front suggestions and to Jonathan Schmidt for keeping everything on schedule. Also, I am indebted to the anonymous copy editors at Tor who ground the rough edges off my prose and punctuation.

My wife, Jean, also provided extensive editing suggestions to clarify many of my answers, which were sometimes too technical for the general reader. She has my gratitude, appreciation, and love for helping with the composition.

Introduction

John H. Glenn, Jr.

Curiosity is a stimulant for learning, and a good question sets the stage for learning at any age. In fact, the ancient philosopher who said "Wisdom begins in wonder" had it about right. Wondering, questioning, learning—they go hand in hand, and the one who answers learns as well as the one who asks.

This book contains many questions that all astronauts have been asked and there seems to be no end to the thirst for knowledge inspired by the wonder of space exploration. It is especially gratifying when our young people become excited by space topics and want to learn more about our world, a world that is expanding far beyond the limits of our home planet.

If your question isn't answered in this book I encourage you to contact the NASA Education Resource Center for your area. They are listed in the back of the book and these offices are eager and willing to provide immediate printout of text, graphics, and pictures for use in school projects.

I urge all readers to develop an inquisitive approach to the world around you. That is the first step toward solving the challenging puzzles and intriguing mysteries of life.

Preface

Many changes have occurred since the last publication of this book and they need to be addressed to update its content. The USSR (Soviet Union) has evolved into the CIS (Commonwealth of Independent States). Their robust space program continues, but with reduced budgets and funding woes. Economic problems also have forced the U.S., Canada, Japan, and European nations to reduce expenditures on space programs. With less money available, programs have been stretched out, many worthwhile efforts have been eliminated, and the necessity for international cooperation for large space ventures has been recognized and implemented.

Begun as an international effort with Canada, Japan, and the European Space Agency, the U.S. Space Station *Freedom* has been modified to include Russian modules and has been renamed as the International Space Station. A vigorous effort has been made to implement compatibility between U.S. and Russian space hardware and mission control centers. Shuttles have docked to the Russian *Mir* space station, astronauts have flown on the *Mir*, cosmonauts have flown on the Shuttle, many astronauts are learning Russian and many cosmonauts are learning English. The NASA Mission Control Center at Houston (MCC) and the Russian Mission Control Center near Moscow (the Kaliningrad TsUP) have open and effective communication links essential to real-time cooperation during joint missions.

Following the enormously successful joint Shuttle-*Mir* missions, confidence has soared in our ability to get the job done together and there is unparalleled optimism about a shared future in space for all nations. When people travel to the space station they will represent many nationalities and all future ambitious programs—such as a manned mission to Mars—will undoubtedly be flown by international crews in spacecraft whose elements were designed and built by workers around the world.

Many new questions have arisen since the last revision of this book. Some address the issues that accompany international efforts and many simply reflect the public's expanding curiosity about life in space or recent discoveries by space crews and satellites. Since the last publication, the Internet has exploded on the scene and many questions have come on the Internet. A new section including Internet and Web addresses has been added to the Appendix.

I'm still amazed and gratified when I get a new question from an audience or by letter from a teacher or student. Many reflect the public's increasing understanding of the more subtle technical, human, economic, and political aspects of space flight. To all the audiences, teachers, schoolchildren, and other correspondents who have provided the questions, I say "Thanks".

Bill Pogue
Bella Vista, Arkansas

HOW DO YOU GO TO THE BATHROOM IN SPACE?

1. How old are you?

I was born in 1930. I was forty-three years old when our mission launched to visit *Skylab*, and I celebrated my forty-fourth birthday while in space

2. What is your academic background?

I have a bachelor of science in secondary education and a master's of science in mathematics, and I taught undergraduate mathematics at the Air Force Academy.

3. Are you a graduate of a service academy?

No, I attended a civilian college and received my commission through the air force aviation cadet program during the Korean conflict.

4. Which branch of the military (service) were you in? How long?

I was in the air force for twenty-five years, nine of which were spent with NASA as an astronaut.

5. What kind of airplanes have you flown?

Over fifty types and models of American and British aircraft, mostly jet fighter aircraft, but including civilian light aircraft, sailplanes, helicopters, open cockpit biplanes of WWII vintage, and four-engine patrol bombers used by the RAF coastal command.

6. What kind of airplane did you fly in Korea?

The F-84G, a fighter-bomber.

7. When did you fly with the Thunderbirds? What airplane did you fly with the aerobatic team? What position?

I flew with the Thunderbirds, the air force aerobatic team, from 1955 to 1957. I flew as solo pilot in the F-84F and F-100C, and slot pilot in the diamond formation for over a year, also in the F-100C.

8. Which do you think was riskier, flying with the Thunderbirds or going into space?

Flying with the Thunderbirds was probably riskier, but I never thought of it as being dangerous because we practiced regularly. The most hazardous flying I ever did was instructing students in aerial gunnery training and air combat maneuvering (dogfighting). Both of these activities involved a lot of airplanes maneuvering close together in the same airspace and it required a lot of attention by the pilots to avoid midair collisions. Inexperienced pilots frequently maneuver in an unpredictable manner, which can create a dangerous situation.

9. Which group of astronauts were you in? When were you selected to be an astronaut? When did you leave the space program?

I was in the fifth group of astronauts selected in 1966 and left the space program in September 1977. I had been turned down on two earlier selections (1961 and 1963) but just kept sending in an application each time NASA announced a selection. I wanted to become an astronaut because it seemed to me to be the highest goal attainable for a pilot as well as being interesting and exciting work.

10. Do you still work on space projects?

I'm on call for work with an aerospace company to provide technical services associated with the International Space Station.

11. How old do you have to be to become an astronaut? At what age do astronauts retire?

No age requirements are stated for selection, nor are astronauts required to retire at any specified age. The average ages at time of selection are about 33–34 for mission specialists (technical/scientific astronauts) and 35–36 for pilot astronauts. The youngest astronaut ever selected was twenty-five, a geologist in the 1967 scientist-astronaut selection (sixth group).

12. Do astronauts have to be pilots?

No. Prior to 1978, all astronauts were required to be pilots or become pilots (through attending air force pilot-training schools). Beginning with the 1978 selection, NASA began selecting in two categories: mission specialist astronaut and pilot astronaut. A third category of astronaut—payload specialist—may be selected for specific flights but they are not career NASA astronauts. Some payload specialists have made several space flights.

13. Do you have to be in a military branch to be an astronaut? How can I become an astronaut?

No, you do not have to be in the military. Civilians have been selected starting with the third group (1963). The first group of scientist astronauts (1964) were all civilians. About 25 percent of each Shuttle astronaut selection are civilians.

Any adult man or woman in excellent physical condition who meets the basic qualifications can be selected to enter astronaut training. The minimum requirements include a bachelor's degree in engineering science or mathematics from an accredited institution with three years of related experience following the degree. Pilots must have 1,000 hours of experience in jet aircraft (most are graduates of a test pilot school). There are 4,000 applications for the twenty openings for selections that are made about every two years. For more information write to the Astronaut Selection Office, NASA Johnson Space Center, Houston, TX 77058 or log onto their Website at: http://38.201.67.70/ shuttle/reference/faq/astronaut.html This site also can be reached through the JSC homepage at: http://www.jsc.nasa.gov

14. How many crews visited _Skylab_? How long did the missions last? What were the names of the other men on your mission? What happened to _Skylab_?

Three crews (three men each) visited _Skylab_ between May 1973 and February 1974. The first crew saved _Skylab_ by performing critical repairs of damage caused during the launch of _Skylab_. They were: Captain Charles E. (Pete) Conrad, commander; Captain Joseph P. (Joe) Kerwin, scientist pilot; and Captain Paul J. Weitz, pilot (twenty-eight days). The second crew was: Captain Alan Bean, commander; Dr. Owen P. Garriott, scientist pilot; and Colonel Jack Lousma, Pilot (fifty-nine days). The other men on my flight (final visit) were Colonel Gerald P. (Jerry) Carr, commander and Dr. Edward G. (Ed) Gibson, scientist pilot (eighty-four days). All three flights set successive endurance records for space flight.

Skylab was put into a "storage" condition when we left it in February 1974, with the intention to service it (for later use) or de-orbit it with a device carried by the Shuttle later in the decade (late 1970s). The choice was left open because it wasn't known if it would be usable after being in space for so long. As it turned out, _Skylab_'s orbit dropped faster than anticipated and it reentered the Earth's atmosphere on July 11, 1979, scattering debris over a path extending eastward from the Indian Ocean to western Australia.

15. What do you think was _Skylab_'s greatest contribution?

The greatest immediate contribution (1974) was the demonstration of man's capability to live and work in weightlessness for long periods (up to three months). The medical/physiological tests and experiments were rigorously performed and documented. They provided the most comprehensive and reliable physiology data on the long-term

Overhead View of *Skylab* **Space Station Cluster with Cloud-Covered Earth in the Background.** This was taken from the *Skylab* 4 Command and Service Module (CSM) on its last orbit before returning home from its final manned mission in February, 1974. (See Question 160.)

physiological effects of space flight for over twenty years. The studies of the Earth and sun provided data for many years of analysis.

16. Why do you need to do astronomy or solar observations from space when it is a lot cheaper and easier to use Earth-based observatories that are already available?

When light from the stars, planets or the sun passes through the Earth's atmosphere, it can create many problems for an astronomer. The light may be entirely blocked or screened out or the light may be changed (distorted) to prevent accurate observations. Studies of the sun's faint outer features, the solar corona, cannot be seen at all because the daytime sky is so bright. On one orbit of *Skylab* more solar corona observations (data) were accumulated than during all previous observations by Earth-based observatories (worldwide). From Earth the corona can only be seen during time of total eclipse of the sun (when the moon passes in front of the sun).

17. Aren't you really thrown back at liftoff? (There is a widespread belief that the astronauts feel their strongest force effect from the engine thrust at the time of liftoff.)

The force on the astronaut at liftoff isn't as great as commonly believed. In the older Saturn boosters, the astronauts were pressed back in the couches at just a bit more than their normal body weight. An astronaut weighing 150 pounds, for instance, would feel like he weighted 165 pounds. On the Space Shuttle, the same astronaut would be pressed back into the seat with a force of about 225 pounds. This is much higher liftoff acceleration than felt on the older boosters, but it isn't nearly the force felt later on during boost.

On Saturn boosters used during the Apollo program the astronauts felt the most force just as the first stage of the rocket had burned up most of its fuel. Just before first-stage shutdown they felt about four times heavier than their normal Earth weight, with the thrust force pressing their backs into the couch. The Space Shuttle thrust is controlled so that the most force the astronauts feel is about three times their normal weight, with the thrust force pressing their bodies into the seat back.

18. How many g's do the Shuttle astronauts feel during reentry? Are the g forces stronger during launch or during entry?

The lower case "g" refers to the force of gravity you feel on Earth. When you sit in a chair your bottom presses down on the seat with a force of 1 g. If you tipped the chair backward so the back was on the floor, your back would be pressing on the chair back with a force of 1 g. When fighter pilots fly in a tight turn they may feel pressed down into the seat with a force as high as seven times their normal weight.

They would call this "pulling 7 g's". When pilots have to use an ejection seat to get out of a crippled airplane, they feel a force of about twenty times the force of normal gravity (20 g's) while the seat shoots out of the aircraft. However, this lasts for less than a second.

Following liftoff, Shuttle astronauts feel the g-force build up gradually to about 3 g's. Then the g-force is kept from getting any higher than 3 g's by throttling back (reducing thrust) of the Shuttle's three large engines. During reentry, the highest force the Shuttle astronauts feel is about 1½ g's, but during reentry the g-force is pressing them down into the seat. They feel the highest g-force during launch.

19. What is the highest g-force any astronaut has felt?

Some of the Apollo astronauts returning from the moon felt the drag force build up to almost 7 g's during reentry through the Earth's atmosphere. This is the most force U.S. astronauts have felt in space flight. However, the highest g-forces of any space flight (as of 1999) were experienced by cosmonauts Vasily Lazarev and Oleg Makarov (April 5, 1975) in their Soyuz spacecraft when the crew was forced to separate from their booster rocket and make an emergency reentry. (The lower core stage of the rocket did not separate completely at staging and wiggled around, causing violent oscillations of the rocket's upper stage.)

The cosmonauts separated from the rocket using their Soyuz spacecraft rocket jettison system and were subjected to a force of 14–15 g's during the reentry.

From Apollo training experience I can say that 14–15 g's is really a heavy load on the body. We were given an "indoctrination" ride in a centrifuge (a simulator cab at the end of a long mechanical arm that slings you around in a circular path). This was done to show us what a reentry would be like if we had a launch problem. All of us were subjected to a 15 g-force to show us the effect. You are really pinned back into the couch and sort of helpless at this g-force level. As the force went above 9 g's I could no longer reach a switch in front of my arm.

BLUE RIDGE LIBRARY
28 AVERY ROW
ROANOKE, VIRGINIA 24012-8828

20. What does it feel like in space?

The first thing you notice when you go into space is an absence of pressure on your body. You may feel light-headed or giddy. After a half hour or so, your face may feel flushed and you might feel a throbbing in your neck. As you move about, you will notice a strong sensation of spinning or tumbling every time you turn or nod your head. This makes some people uncomfortable or nauseated. You will also have a very "full feeling" or stuffiness in your head. You may get a bad headache after a few hours, and this too may make you feel sick to your stomach.

Most all of these symptoms will go away in a few days. The head congestion or stuffiness may bother you off and on during your entire time in space. Throughout the space flight, you will feel a powerful sensation of tumbling or spinning every time you move your head too fast.

There are two things you can do on Earth to get a reasonable idea what it feels like in space. The general floating feeling is quite similar to the effect of relaxing in a swimming pool. The head stuffiness experienced in space is much like the uncomfortable feeling that one gets when hanging upside-down from gymnast bars. Normally, it is uncomfortable to stay in this position beyond a minute or two because of the full feeling in the head caused by the upside-down position.

21. How long does it take to get used to space?

It takes the body about three days to adjust or adapt to the weightlessness. You will become accustomed to working in space in a few hours, but you will be learning better ways to do things throughout the mission. Even though I got sick the first evening in space, the following day—which was our first full day in orbit—I worked fourteen hours.

22. When sailors go to sea, they gradually get their "sea legs." Did you get "space legs" after being in space for a while?

We did, quite literally, develop space legs. We called it "bird legs," because our legs became thinner and thinner as the weeks passed.

BIRDLEGS

The calves, in particular, became quite small. During the first few days in space, the legs become smaller because the muscles of the legs force blood and other fluids toward the upper part of the body, thus decreasing the girth measurement around the thighs and calves. In addition, muscle tissue is progressively lost owing to insufficient exercise. These changes produce a "bird leg" effect. Shuttle astronauts notice this effect even though their flights are relatively short.

23. What happened to your body in space?

We grew $1\frac{1}{2}$–$2\frac{1}{4}$ inches taller. This height increase was owed to spinal lengthening and straightening. The discs between the vertebrae

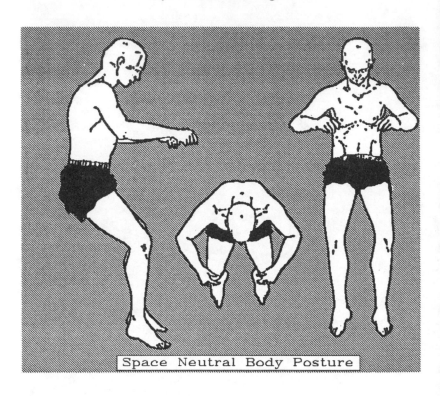

Space Neutral Body Posture

expand and compress slightly, depending on the weight the back is supporting. Even on Earth, an adult will be slightly taller (about ½ inch) in the morning than in the evening because the discs expand during sleep and compress as you walk or sit during the day. In weightlessness, the discs expand, but they don't compress again, because there is never weight on the spine. Our space suits were custom-tailored on Earth to our height and posture, thus, they fit tighter in space because of the height increase. Also, my waist measurement decreased by almost three inches, owing to an upward shift of the internal organs in the body creating a "wasp waist" appearance. After return to Earth the height and waist measurements returned to normal.

In addition to the height increase and waist thinning, the posture changes slightly. Your relaxed body posture is semi-erect with the knees slightly bent, head tilted forward, shoulders up (similar to a

WE LOST ALL OF THE HEIGHT

shrug), and arms floating up and bent in at the elbows with hands in front at about chest height. This posture is referred to as "space neutral body posture."

There is one confusing aspect of these changes. Although the body "length" is greater, the "effective body height" is actually less than on Earth because of the semi-crouch assumed by the relaxed body.

Because of the raised position of the arms, it was an effort to work for long periods at waist height as you ordinarily do; you must continually bend forward and force your arms down to waist level to do work at "table height."

Also, you can't remain in a seated position without a belt to hold your body down in the seat. The body's tendency to resume the semi-erect space neutral body posture makes it necessary to exert continuous effort with the abdominal muscles to stay "bent forward." If you flex your body to get into a chair, and then relax, you'll pop right out of the chair.

We found it much easier to pull our legs upward to lace our shoes rather than bend down. Inability to bend forward easily also made it harder to get the upper part of the one-piece space suits over our heads. We put our legs in from the opening in the back of the suit and then had to bend forward while we lifted the top half of the suit over our head to get our heads through the neck ring. Shuttle astronauts don't have this problem because their suits are two-piece joined at a waist ring.

24. Do you look the same in space?

No, facial appearance changes quite a lot. I was really surprised— if not shocked—the first time I looked in the mirror; I didn't look like me anymore. Loose flesh on the face rises, or floats, on the bone structure, giving a high-cheekboned or Asian appearance. The face also looks a bit puffy, with bags under the eyes, especially during the first few days, and the veins in your forehead and neck appear swollen.

After about three or four days, some of the facial puffiness (edema) and vein enlargement goes away, but your face still looks quite a bit different. Incidentally, for safety the mirrors we used were made of stainless steel instead of glass. In weightlessness, pieces of broken glass would float around and create a serious threat to the astronauts.

25. Did you gain or lose weight? If you were weightless, how could you weigh yourself?

We lost about three or four pounds during the first four days of the mission. Then we gradually regained most of the loss, so that, by the

WE GREW TALLER

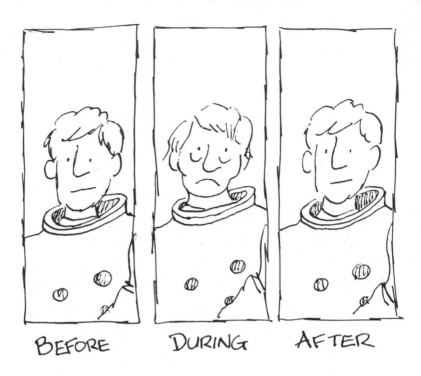

BEFORE   DURING   AFTER

end of the mission (eighty-four days), we were just about back to our weight at launch. Most of the early flight weight loss is caused by elimination (reduction) of body fluids. The fluid shift causes excessive fluids in the upper half of the body; the body senses these localized excesses and reduces the total body fluid through urination.

We really didn't weigh ourselves the same way you do on Earth because a spring or balance scale wouldn't work. However, we could determine body mass, and then convert this to an equivalent Earth weight, by sitting in a special chair that swung back and forth on springs. The time it took for each swing of the chair was measured and used by a computer to determine our body mass, or Earth weight. This device was called a *body mass measurement device* (BMMD). Shuttle astronauts use an improved version of the BMMD on flights devoted to medical/physiological studies.

I found the device mildly unpleasant because the metal was cold and we used it the first thing after waking up, while we were still in

LIVE AND WORK IN
WEIGHTLESSNESS

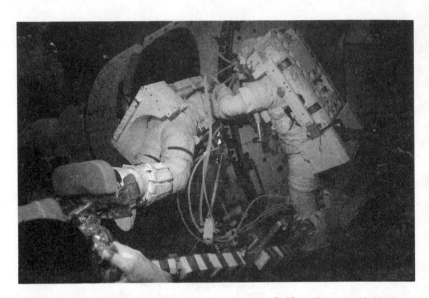

STS-88 Training View   Astronauts Jerry L. Ross (left) and James H. Newman training in the Neutral Buoyancy Laboratory (NBL). The large boxlike addition at the bottom of the EMU backpack is the Simplified Aid for EVA Rescue (SAFER) unit. It's a really small jetpack that allows the astronaut to manevuer back to the spacecraft in an emergency.

our underwear. The chair was actually more like a box, and we had to get in it with our knees doubled up under our chin. This jammed-up position was required to reduce body fluid slosh and internal organ movement in our bodies during the oscillations of the chair. Minimizing this "body slosh" was necessary to get an accurate reading with the device. We had two smaller devices for measuring biological samples and food residue (what we didn't eat). The small unit was called a *specimen mass measurement device* (SMMD) and could handle items less than one pound mass.

26. Is it true that you lost a lot of calcium from your bones and that this may make long missions impossible?

This is partly correct. We did lose calcium from the bones, but it wasn't excessive. After *Skylab*, NASA doctors worried that this loss might become bad enough on long space flights to cause serious harm to the skeletons of astronauts. Estimates based on *Skylab* data showed that bone-mass loss would be 6–7 percent for a year-long stay in weightlessness.

Since then the Russians have completed progressively longer missions leading up to a yearlong mission aboard their *Mir* space station in 1987 and 1988. In 1995 a cosmonaut completed a flight of almost fifteen months. The cosmonauts exercised diligently, completing two one-hour exercise periods per day using a treadmill and stationary bicycle. It appears that this has stemmed the calcium loss.

The calcium loss is similar to that experienced by bed-rest patients on Earth. Such patients show a marked decrease in the rate of calcium loss after the first few months of being bedridden. People over forty also experience calcium loss from the bones (osteoporosis). One view of the space loss is that it is also self-limiting, i.e., the loss rate drops off after several months in weightlessness. After twenty-five years I have had no ill effects (skeletal problems) from a three-month stay.

27. Why don't you just take calcium supplements (tablets) to balance the calcium loss?

At the time of *Skylab* this would not have worked because taking heavy doses of calcium would not have helped the problem and could have led to the formation of kidney stones. A few years ago a new medication was developed called *sodium alendronate*. By taking this along with calcium supplements, patients have been able to correct the calcium loss or osteoporosis.

There appear to be three general approaches to controlling the calcium loss without the aid of medication:

1. Exercise countermeasures as practiced on *Skylab, Salyut*, and *Mir* space stations.
2. The use of calcium supplements (previously described).
3. Artificial gravity countermeasures that involve periodic exposure to force generated in a rotating device called a *centrifuge*, or long-term exposure to the same type of force generated by rotating the entire spacecraft assembly.

Despite the Russian experience, NASA is taking a cautious approach to this problem, is studying all three options above, and is planning rigorous medical and physiological tests for International Space Station (ISS) crew members.

28. What would happen if you got a bone broken in space? Would it knit (heal) properly?

We were trained to treat the problem by attaching a splint; we wouldn't have tried to set the bone because we didn't have the training or the equipment such as X-ray machines.

The question of bone healing has not been encountered because no crew members have broken a bone in space. Breaking a bone in space is highly unlikely. However, we need to understand more about the basic process of bone tissue restoration before this question can be answered.

Tests performed on rats during a 1990 Shuttle flight produced results that indicated that an untended fracture may not heal properly. The concern is that the bone would not heal with sufficient strength to handle the loads and forces that would be encountered upon return to Earth. However, there are ways to induce proper healing even in space, such as the simulation of Earth forces by exercises and exercise equipment.

29. Do you get tired in space?

Yes, we did get tired in weightlessness. Heavy exercise left us with a comfortable, tired feeling. We also experienced a psychological weariness from rushing to keep on schedule. All astronauts on *Skylab* have reported a sort of overall tiredness, a fatigue or rundown feeling, that often occurred about three or four hours after eating. The *Skylab* astronauts called it "space crud." It's sort of like the down-and-out feeling you have when you're coming down with a bad cold or the flu. I still don't understand what caused this, but we learned very quickly

Bad Hair Day?   Or just another day in gravity-free space? Astronaut Marsha S. Ivins, mission specialist, onboard the Earth-orbiting Space Shuttle *Columbia*. Question: What do you call tangled hair in space? Answer: astro*knots*.

that it was unwise to skip meals to save time. If we did, we would begin to feel bad and were much more likely to make a mistake.

I noticed one peculiar inconsistency about the space crud: I didn't develop it on space walks, even though I went for six to seven hours without eating or drinking. I don't know why the effects should be absent on space walks, unless it was because we enjoyed it so much that it helped to offset the occurrence of those type of symptoms.

30. Does your hair float out from your head?

Yes. Our hair was short enough that this wasn't a problem. It appears from mission video and photos, that medium-length curled hair is also manageable but the hair does extend out from the head more than on Earth. Long, straight hair and slightly wavy hair spreads out and—from the flight scenes aboard Shuttle—it looks like it could present a problem; it's easy to get things snagged in weightlessness. I noticed from studying postflight films that female astronauts with

U.S. International Cooperation Phase III   A Space Shuttle is docked to the International Space Station (ISS) in this computer-generated representation of the United States' international cooperation in space. Phase III of the ISS is depicted here in its completed and fully operational state with elements from the United States, Europe, Canada, Japan and Russia. In the Shuttle cargo bay is the Italian Space Agency (ASI) Mini Pressurized Logistics Module (IMPLM). The IMPLM will be used to resupply payloads and to return payloads to Earth. Artwork done by John Frassanito and Associates.

long hair use varying methods to manage their hair, sometimes letting it float free and other times rolling it into a bun or tying it in a sort of ponytail.

31. How did you breathe? Was breathing any different?

The spacecraft is pressurized or filled with air; on *Skylab* space walks the space suit was inflated by a steady flow of air supplied through a long hose called an *umbilical*. The continuous flow made sure there was always fresh air in the suit. Suits used by Shuttle astronauts contain an oxygen supply in tanks attached to the back of the suit and the astronauts are not attached to the Shuttle by a hose or an umbilical.

Although we didn't notice any difference, tests (vital capacity tests) made on *Skylab* showed we couldn't breathe as deeply (inhale as much air) as during preflight tests. In weightlessness, there is a noticeable shift of the abdominal organs upward toward the rib cage. This may have been the reason it was harder to breathe as deeply.

32. How did you avoid high humidity from building up in the air, owing to respiration and evaporation from the body?

The air inside *Skylab* was circulated across cold metal plates where the water vapor condensed and was then collected and transferred into a waste-water tank. The device was called a *condensing heat exchanger*. The Shuttle and Space Station use a similar system. On *Skylab* this system was very effective and the air was usually quite dry, about the same as a desert climate.

However, in smaller volumes and with more crew members onboard, humidity buildup can be a problem. During short-mission crew visits when there are six cosmonauts on the *Mir* space station, spokesmen have reported an increase in the temperature and humidity. As the Russians have added more modules (volume) to the *Mir* this has been much less of a problem; the growth modules have increased overall systems capacity including humidity control.

33. What kind of soap did you use?

We used both bar and liquid soap (shampoo). It was similar to Neutrogena. The bar soap had a disc of iron in it so it would stick to magnetic posts in the hand-wash area. Astronauts on the Shuttle use Ivory soap.

34. What is warp (space warp)?

Space warp is the imaginary concept of science fiction writers. It is envisioned as a way of getting from one place to another without crossing the distance between them. At the present time, no one is able to achieve such a thing as space warp.

35. How did you get from one place to another inside the spacecraft?

Inside *Skylab*, we pulled ourselves along structural surfaces by using handholds (special handgrips or handles) or other parts of the spacecraft; we also shoved or pushed off from one position to float to the next location. When shoving off to float across a large empty volume, we went headfirst, feetfirst, and also sideways—launching ourselves in a manner to keep from tumbling en route. We were usually able to arrive at the next location in the best position to grasp and hold fixtures. In small volumes, however, we had to be careful to avoid damage to the spacecraft when we moved around. Headfirst motion was the one used most often.

The "floors" of two of the large compartments in *Skylab* consisted of an open triangular grid or mesh; our shoes had a special triangular cleat on the sole of the shoe that fitted into the triangular holes in the grid, and locked into position by a twist of the foot. These were used to hold us in position at work sites. As an experiment, I replaced the triangles with mushroom-shaped metal cones and tried to "walk" across the grid by hooking the edge of the mushroom in the grid openings. It didn't work; every time I stretched out my foot to take the next step, my foot just floated in the air and I had to exert considerable effort to get my foot down toward the floor grid. It was a lot harder than just floating across the area.

Shuttle and Space Station astronauts use the same techniques for moving around in the Shuttle and Space Station. They are most always in reach of a grasping surface, can move easily within the modules, and prefer wearing socks because their foot restraints are foot loops. Space Station astronauts have a variety of foot restraints to use and some can be mounted on the rack handrails for jobs that require a long time at the work site.

36. How did you get between locations on the outside of *Skylab*?

Moving around outside the spacecraft requires greater care. On an EVA (*extravehicular activity* or "space walk"), transfer handholds and

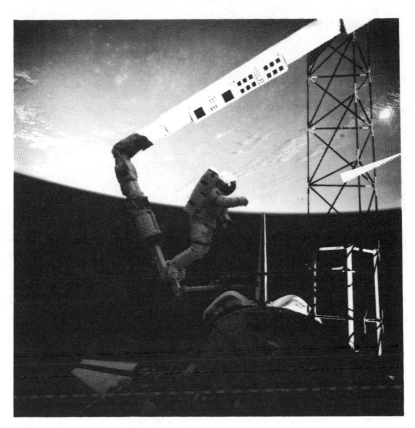

Space Shuttle Extravehicular Activity (EVA)   Astronaut Jerry L. Ross, during a 1986 mission, approaches an experimental tower to be used to test construction techniques in outer space.

other aids were essential in getting from one place to another. Foot restraints were located at all planned work stations so that the astronaut didn't have to hold onto something continually in order to maintain position. Transfer handholds were often similar to the rungs of a ladder and were spaced for moving hand-over-hand to travel between locations.

Shuttle and Space Station astronauts on EVA have other aids in addition to handholds and foot restraints. A cable is attached along one edge of the payload bay. EVA crew members can attach a tether (strap) from their suit to the wire using a hook on the end of the tether. Thus secured, they can move the full length of the payload bay (sixty feet) without handholds. They also have a device that fits to the end of the remote manipulator system (robot arm) called a *manipulator foot restraint* (MFR). When a Shuttle astronaut gets into this movable foot restraint, the robot arm can move and position the astronaut for work throughout a large area around the Shuttle. EVA astronauts on the Space Station will have MFRs that can be attached to the Station's robot arm (SSRMS—space station remote manipulator system). The SSRMS is attached to a platform called the MSB (mobile servicer base). The MSB is attached to the Station truss structure and can move along the truss to reposition itself for various work sites along the truss.

For early Shuttle missions, the Shuttle astronauts sometimes used a *manned maneuvering unit* (MMU). The MMU is actually a miniature spacecraft that can be flown free of the Shuttle by a suited crew member. (The Shuttle suits include self-contained life support systems and do not require a hose connection to the Shuttle.) The MMU greatly increased the work capability of astronauts, enabling them to fly out from the Shuttle to inspect satellites and dock (attach) to them. The control system of the MMU was then used to maneuver the satellite back to the Shuttle for repair on orbit, or return to Earth for repair or analysis. Currently, the MMU is not being maintained ready for flight because of the expense involved.

For the Shuttle and International Space Station a new, less bulky jetpack with limited maneuvering capability has been developed for use during space walks. It is called the SAFER (*simplified aid for EVA rescue*). In the event that an astronaut becomes accidentally disconnected from a tether (restraint rope) or foot restraint, the SAFER will enable the astronauts to use the small thrusters or engines on the SAFER to maneuver back to the Shuttle or Space Station. The SAFER fits to the bottom of the suit backpack and has hand controls on each side behind each hip. The SAFER also has an automatic control feature to stop rotations if the astronaut develops a tumble when drifting away.

Skylab Space Walk Scientist-Astronaut Owen K. Garriot, science pilot on the second *Skylab* mission, is performing Extravehicular Activity (EVA or, "space walk") at the Apollo Telescope Mount of the *Skylab* space station in Earth orbit.

37. What kind of work did you do on *Skylab*?

Skylab was an experimental space station and we operated equipment and instruments for more than fifty experiments. The three principal experiments were performed throughout the mission and occupied a lot of time each day. We had a solar observatory for making observations of the sun, cameras, and other instruments for studying the Earth, and equipment for several medical experiments to determine

WE DIDN'T HAVE THE RIGHT TOOLS

the long-term effects of weightlessness on the human body. We also changed filters, replaced drive motors on tape recorders, did housekeeping chores such as vacuuming filter screens, and repaired broken equipment.

38. What kinds of problems did you have in doing repair work?

Some of the repair jobs were really crude because we didn't have the right tools or materials. Ed Gibson operated one instrument that used batteries to power a light inside to create a sighting reference on a mirror surface. The batteries kept running down and Ed had to keep installing fresh batteries. Finally, he ran out of spare batteries, so he had to dig out some other batteries that were intended for our tape recorders, and try to make them work. They didn't fit in the instrument, so he had to run wires from the inside of the instrument and tape them on the battery terminals. It worked, but it really looked weird.

The clump of batteries sort of floated on the end of the wires, and Ed finally had to tape the whole glob on the side of the instrument.

THE SCREW WOULDN'T TURN —
YOU WOULD

Ed said we were bumping into the batteries and loosening the wires. I was surprised that the tape held the wires snugly enough against the battery terminals to make a good electrical connection. Early in *Skylab* training we had asked for a soldering iron as a part of our tool kit, but the mission planners said there was no need for one and disapproved the request. As it turned out, a soldering iron would have been very useful when Ed rigged his battery assembly.

39. Was it hard work?

Yes. Some tasks were very difficult, but most were routine and merely took time. The hardest jobs were repair and maintenance tasks that involved a lot of physical force, such as pulling or twisting. Sometimes there was no convenient surface or handgrip to hold onto with the free hand to keep from floating or swaying when we handled equipment.

A typical problem we faced was in trying to loosen or tighten screws on a large flat surface. When using tools requiring a lot of force like screwdrivers or socket wrenches, it was necessary to have your body firmly restrained or tied down before applying force; otherwise, when you applied force, your body would move instead of the wrench. For example, if you floated over to a panel, inserted a screwdriver into the slot of a screw, and twisted your wrist, the screw wouldn't turn—you would! To apply a strong twist force, you normally have to push on the screwdriver while twisting it. In doing one repair job, I found it necessary to rig pull straps for my left hand so I could pull to balance the push force of my right hand. If you're patient and aren't pressed for time, these problems become an interesting challenge. If you're trying to meet a critical time schedule, it can be very irritating and frustrating.

On the average, we figured it took about twice the time to do a job in weightlessness than it took on Earth. One particular servicing task I did was extremely hard to do even on the ground. It involved reaching into an enclosed area to disconnect and reconnect two plumbing lines by sliding metal sleeves on pipes that ran sideways to my arm direction. I only had to do it once in space, but that was enough. My legs were thrashing around as I tried to get my arms in the best position, and when I finally finished, my wrists were scratched and cut from banging into the sheet-metal edges around the access opening. I really felt "pooped" by the end of the day. You can't "stretch yourself" like you can on Earth when you keep going to finish a long job.

Shuttle astronauts have performed many unplanned maintenance and repair tasks such as changing out display devices (similar to a TV screen) and rewiring complex experiment instruments. Many of the mission specialists and payload specialists have helped in the design of Shuttle instruments and have the knowledge and skills to do repair work that we would never have tried during earlier space programs.

40. What did you do on space walks?

On space walks (EVAs), we changed film magazines in the solar telescopes (seventy-five Earth pounds each), mounted instruments for solar studies, carried out a large camera to photograph a comet (Kohotek), installed and removed test samples to evaluate the effect of space on materials, photographed the outside of the *Skylab*, and retrieved experiment equipment installed by the previous crew. Repair jobs included modifying the drive mechanism of a radar antenna used for Earth studies and unjamming the filter wheel of a solar telescope.

Shuttle astronauts have conducted space walks that required much more complicated training and equipment and the handling of massive satellites. Throughout the 1980s and 1990s they have repaired scientific and communications satellites weighing up to a ton and in December 1993 they repaired the Hubble Space Telescope (HST) in a series of space walks. These were the most difficult space walk tasks ever done and required the careful removal and installation of optical and electronic components inside the telescope. If they had bumped the parts too hard it could have damaged the components or ruined the precise alignment of the telescope parts. In February 1996 Shuttle crew members added new equipment to the HST in a series of space walks.

Space Station astronauts will be heavily involved during the assembly of the station, and later during servicing and maintenance jobs that require space walks. The International Space Station is designed for a fifteen-year service life and it will require many servicing and repair jobs.

41. Was it hard to work while in a space suit?

Yes. It was hard work. The suit is bulky and stiff, which makes it difficult to bend or turn your body. The gloves are very thick, so you don't have much feel. Because air pressure in the gloves tends to hold the fingers out straight, it is very tiring to maintain a grip on anything. I always felt like a "bull in a china closet" when working in a space suit. After doing a lot of work in a suit, my fingertips became very sore and tender and I had cuts and burns on my shoulders from the braided metal arm-support cables inside the suit. Even so, we enjoyed the space walks and looked forward to the chance to get outside. I was out on a space walk once for six and a half hours and once for seven hours.

The suits used by Shuttle astronauts provide better torso mobility (twisting at the waist). The arms and legs are a bit easier to move and the suit is easier to put on, although they still cannot don the suit without assistance. However, the gloves are not much better than the older designs; hand and finger movement still require a lot of effort and arm/hand fatigue are still experienced. In addition, the Shuttle astronauts have noticed that their hands get too cold when working for long periods in the dark or in shaded positions out of sunlight. The glove has been modified to include heating elements to keep the hands warm and, during a recent Shuttle space walk test, the astronauts gave it a hearty approval.

NASA has tested two new suit designs, each designed to work at a higher pressure, with the objective to improve overall body mobility and hand dexterity (better glove). The higher pressure is desired to reduce the time a suited astronaut must wait before entering and depressurizing the airlock prior to going outside into the space vacuum. In going from a high pressure to a low pressure, dissolved gasses (nitrogen) in the blood tend to "fizz" out (come out of solution); this is similar to what happens to a soda when the cap or tab is removed from the container. When this action takes place in a person's body, the nitrogen bubbles can cause several problems: The one most familiar is the "bends" that scuba divers or deep-sea divers experience when they come up too fast from deep dives. To reduce this possibility, astronauts breathe 100 percent oxygen for a period of time to remove the nitrogen from their blood (a bit comes out from the lungs each time they exhale).

The length of time needed to do this depends on the difference between the spacecraft cabin pressure and the operating pressure of the suit—the higher the suit pressure the less time to get the nitrogen level down to an acceptable concentration. Cutting down this oxygen "pre-breathe" time is desired to reduce the time lost just waiting, and to enable the astronauts to get outside more quickly in the event emergency work is required on the outside of the spacecraft. However, for the first several years astronauts on the International Space Station will be using the same suits they now use on the Shuttle.

42. Would a person without legs be able to work in space?

Based on my experience, I feel that such a person would be able to work quite effectively in the weightless condition. Virtually all of the work in space is done with the arms and hands. The feet and legs are used mainly for holding you in position at a work location and for shoving yourself from one location to another. However, you also can move yourself quite easily by using arms and hands.

43. When you were on a space walk, did you work during darkness?

Yes, we normally worked during darkness. In Earth orbit at altitudes from 120–500 miles, the time for one complete orbit is approximately ninety minutes (slightly longer for higher orbits; slightly less for lower orbits). Generally, about fifty minutes are in sunlight and forty minutes in darkness.

We had no difficulty working in areas where lighting was provided. Some repair work had to be done in locations where no lighting had been installed because the designers had not expected a problem would occur there. In those locations we had to stop work when it got dark. Sometimes it started getting dark right in the middle of a long task and created a problem as we tried to "button up" the work area to wait for sunrise. Although darkness occurs quickly in space, we usually had ample warning because the Earth below us got dark a few minutes before we flew out of the sunlight.

Shuttle astronauts have lights mounted on their helmets and the same will be true for Space Station astronauts. These lights are a great improvement because they shine light directly on the area you are facing. This will be a great advantage for the Space Station because it is so large and it will be impossible to provide outside lighting for all parts of the station.

44. What did you do if your nose itched when you were in the space suit?

Not only did my nose itch occasionally, but also my ears. Because a scratch is almost an involuntary reaction, I frequently reached up to scratch my nose and hit my helmet—which can make you feel really dumb. I scratched my nose by rubbing it on a little nose-pincher device we used to clear our ears.

If our ears stopped up or became uncomfortable owing to pressure changes in the suit, the procedure was to press the nose against this open V device in order to hold our nostrils closed while we exerted a slight blowing pressure. This is a common technique used by fliers to clear their ears. If our ears itched, we just had to tolerate it. I usually tried rubbing the side of my head against the inside of the helmet, but it didn't help much. The best thing to do was to think of something else.

45. Was it quiet or noisy in space?

Sound can't travel through space because there is no air to carry the sound waves. However, there was a moderate noise level inside *Skylab*, most of which was caused by pumps, fans, and voice chatter on the radio. We had a teleprinter that made a pecking sound similar to a typewriter—this made it difficult to sleep at times. Occasionally, small thrusters on the outside of *Skylab* would fire, which sounded like someone hammering on a large piece of metal.

The most peculiar sound we noticed was a deep rumble that occurred about every forty-five minutes. It sounded like the roll of distant thunder. Jerry asked, "Is it just me or do you hear a rumble every hour or so?" We all agreed that we heard it and finally decided it was owed to alternate heating and cooling of the side of *Skylab* that faced the sun. This surface expanded as it heated up and shrank (contracted) as it cooled. The noise created was similar to the crackling sound made by a furnace or woodstove as it heats up or cools down. The total structure of *Skylab* was so large that it produced a low-pitched rumble instead of a crackling noise. The most disturbing noise on *Skylab* was a loud squeal from the intercom system that occurred when the system wasn't adjusted properly.

ISS Canadian SSRMS Artist's Conception This artist's conception depicts the Canadian Space Station Remote Manipulator System (SSRMS) mechanical arm aboard the International Space Station (ISS). Attached to the end of the arm is the Special Purpose Dexterous Manipulator (SPDM), or "Canada Hand," also being developed for the station.

Astronauts who have flown on *Skylab* and the Shuttle have commented that the Shuttle is much noisier. The Shuttle cabin volume is smaller than *Skylab* and it has more pumps and fans in a smaller area. Keeping the noise level down is a major objective of designers working on the International Space Station. It will be interesting to see if the Space Station creaks, groans, and rumbles as it passes into and out of darkness.

46. What kind of tools did you have?

Because of the long missions scheduled on *Skylab*, it was thought that we would need an assortment of tools to repair breakdowns in equipment. We had a rather complete set of light tools, and we used most of them at one time or the other. Most of the tools were bought at hardware stores, but some were specially made for anticipated repair work. The tools included various types of screwdrivers and pliers, socket wrenches, and torque wrenches. Special tool kits were also provided for repair jobs on space walks. Each astronaut had pockets in his trousers to carry a Swiss army knife and a pair of surgical scissors, which were used frequently for minor repair work.

Many new tools have been added during the Shuttle era. Portable power tools have greatly reduced the time and effort required to remove and replace fasteners (screws, bolts, nuts). Socket tools have special locks to prevent loss of sockets during EVA work (space walks).

The manipulator foot restraint (MFR) attached to the RMS (robot arm) can be fitted with a portable work station. The portable work station is an open framework in front of the EVA crew member when his feet are in the foot restraints of the MFR. It serves as a handhold and also a tool "caddie" to store the tools and keep them in easy reach. The Space Station will require a lot more special tools because of the complicated assembly tasks and planned or unplanned repair requirements that will arise both inside and outside the station.

47. Did you ever lose anything?

Yes. Several items were lost and never found. Frequently, our tableware, usually a knife, would get knocked off the magnetized surface on our food trays. The air flow in *Skylab* would usually carry the items to a filter screen in the air duct system, where they would stick owing to the slight vacuum. This was the first place we looked when something was missing.

One day, when I whirled around to get a camera to take a picture of Hawaii, my eyeglasses flew off. I heard them bouncing around through the experiment compartment as I was taking the picture, but when I went to get them, I couldn't find them. Three days later, Dr. Gibson found them floating near the ceiling in his sleep compartment.

I had a spare set of half-specs—granny glasses—which I used until Ed found my bifocals. I didn't like the half-specs because the straight earpieces allowed the lenses to float up off my nose and bob up and down in front of my eyes. It was very distracting when I was using both hands to do a job. Current astronauts have elastic eyeglass restraints to prevent this "bobbing" problem. Also, astronauts now have the option of using contact lenses. (See Question 70.)

48. How did you clean the spacecraft, or did you have to clean the spacecraft?

As on Earth, a lot of trash accumulated during the day (food packaging, tissues, wet wipes, dirty towels, and washcloths). Most of this was immediately shoved through a push-through slot into a waste container. However, bits of skin, fingernails, hair, food crumbs, odd pieces of paper, and the like tended to drift around and eventually were sucked up against air filters. We used vacuum cleaners to clean off the filters, and that took care of most of the problem. The worst mess was in the area where we ate. Small drops of liquid from our drinks and crumbs from our food would float around until they stuck on the wall or in an open-grid ceiling above our food table, and it became quite dirty. Although we could see into this ceiling area, we couldn't get our hands in to wipe it clean, so it became progressively worse throughout the mission. Near the end of the flight, it began to look like the bottom of a birdcage. I just stopped looking at the ceiling after a while because it was such a mess.

Every two weeks we had to wipe down the walls and surfaces of the toilet with a biocide (disinfectant) to prevent a buildup of microorganisms (germs, mold, etc.). Periodic cleaning of this type will be required for the International Space Station, to prevent a gradual buildup of biologically active contamination. This will be a time-consuming procedure but will be essential to preserve a healthy environment for the Space Station astronauts. Even on the short Shuttle missions, astronauts clean several areas that are exposed to contamination, especially food and drink spills. Overall, Shuttle cleanup is done by the ground crews between missions.

49. Did you write? How did you write?

I found that a lot of writing became an irritating task in weightlessness, particularly when it had to be done on narrow strips

Shuttle Teleprinter   Shuttle Commander Dick Truly reading from a long scroll from the teleprinter. Taking notes onboard the Shuttle was not as easy as one might think. The use of computer notebooks has made the job a lot easier.

of paper that came out of our teleprinter. This paper was just a bit wider than the paper used in cash registers. It tended to curl up and was hard to hold steady on a flat surface. We often used the food-tray tops, our dinner table, as a desk, and we had to exert effort to bend forward to get into a good position to write. Also, we had to hold downward force to keep our hands and arms down on the table while writing. Other astronauts didn't seem to mind this as much as I did.

The teleprinter on the Shuttle uses roll paper eight inches wide. Normal clipboards can be used to hold the paper for easy reference and provides a hand rest for making notes. The addition of portable notebook computers and the uplink of data to the Shuttle has reduced the note-taking chores. The portable computers were carried on all Shuttle missions starting with Shuttle mission STS-63 and accept customized hard drives for both standard and specialized crew tasks.

On the Space Station much of the information will be displayed electronically on flat panel displays of laptop computers that can be connected to data ports located throughout the various modules. However, there will very likely still be a need to use "hard copy" (paper) for various purposes.

50. Did you use pen or pencil?

We used mechanical pencils, pressurized ballpoint pens that assured ink flow in weightlessness, and felt-tip pens. The ballpoints and mechanical pencils worked well, but the felt-tips dried out very quickly in the low humidity of *Skylab*, so they weren't of much use.

Pencil leads did break off, but they didn't cause any problems, even though it would have been possible to get a piece in the eye—or inhale it. These small bits of pencil lead were carried by airflow and collected on intake filter screens.

51. How did you keep a book open to the right page?

This occasionally became a real problem. Most of our flight documents were printed on stiff paper and held together by metal rings that could be opened to insert or remove pages. We had clips to hold the books open to the right page, but they didn't attach very tightly and occasionally they would pop off and the whole book would fan open—costing us considerable time in relocating the right page. The covers were made of extra-heavy paper to make it easy to find the front of the book and the index. When reading a book from our personal library, which was mostly paperbacks, we held the book with one hand, with our thumb in the open crease, and dog-eared the pages to mark our place.

Shuttle astronauts have CRTs (functionally the same as TV picture tubes) that display text, graphic, and video pictures. They also use conventional hard-copy (printed) checklists similar to the books described above.

WATER IN A DRINKING GLASS WOULD TEND TO CRAWL UP

52. How did free water behave in weightlessness?

In weightlessness, water and other thin liquids must be fully enclosed in a container to prevent them from spilling and floating around. If you could get water in a normal drinking glass, it would tend to crawl up the inside surface, over the edge, and down the outside of the glass. Free water droplets become spherical or ball-shaped. Large drops or balls of water quiver and jiggle like gelatin as they float about. On *Skylab*, we performed many science demonstrations with water drops.

One of the most fascinating effects with drops of water was created by injecting air in large water drops, using a hypodermic syringe.

Starting with a drop of water about two inches across, I injected air into the center—it became a hollow ball. I tried to make it larger by squirting more air into the center but missed the center and injected it into the water shell surrounding the hollow core. It formed a second hollow ball joined to the first with a flat surface between them. After a third injection it looked like a Mickey Mouse head. They were really water drop models of complex geometric shapes. Later on I regretted not taking pictures of them.

53. Did you bring food, clothes, etc. with you when you went to visit *Skylab*? What kind of food did you eat?

When *Skylab* was launched it contained all the food, water, clothes, and repair parts for the three planned missions. Originally, our mission had been planned for fifty-six days so we brought a twenty-eight-day supply of food (food bars, some freeze-dried foods—and drinks) to supplement the fifty-six-day supply already on board *Skylab*. We also brought enough underwear and socks for the extra month.

In addition to these supplies for the scheduled eighty-four days, we had a two-week supply of food and water stashed in our command module. This supply would have allowed us to wait two weeks for rescue if we had to make an emergency undocking from *Skylab*, and then had a problem with the command module. The command module, our "ferry spacecraft," was a modified Apollo spacecraft and it had been originally designed for a two-week stay in space. After being docked to *Skylab* and virtually inactive for twelve weeks, we weren't sure what kind of problems might be encountered after we undocked.

Each astronaut selected his menu items from a shopping list of seventy-two food items prepared by commercial companies and NASA dietitians. We had dehydrated vegetables, scrambled eggs, and spaghetti. After adding water and heating them, most were quite good. We had canned puddings, fruit (peaches, pears) and dried fruit (apricots). In addition to freeze-dried food such as salmon, for the first time in space we had frozen food, which included steak, prime rib, pork, and ice cream. We had no bread or milk. We also had a wide variety of drinks, which included orange, grapefruit, strawberry, cherry, grape, and coffee and tea.

The only food that was a disappointment was the chili. I was really looking forward to having it, but the oil separated from the meat and sauce and it looked very unappetizing when we opened the can. I stirred it up as much as I could and jammed my crackers into the can before eating it.

Shuttle astronauts have over 100 food and drink items from which they can select their food. An average daily diet is about 3,000 calories, consisting of 20 percent protein, 50 percent carbohydrates (starches), and 30 percent fat.

Space Station crews will include astronauts from many countries of Western Europe, Japan, Russia, and Canada as well as diverse regions of the United States. The food selections will have to accommodate the tastes and preferences of astronauts from many different cultures. For instance, the typical Japanese diet is higher in protein and lower in fat than a typical American or European diet.

54. How did you keep frozen food frozen?

There was a food freezer on *Skylab*, which was kept below freezing by coolant chilled in a radiator on the outside at the rear of the Space Station. We had the same problem with frost inside the freezer as you have here on Earth, and we had to remove the frost frequently. We used wet cloths to melt the ice around the door and on the inside. We soaked up as much of the frost as we could and then squeezed the cold water out of the washcloth in a special device that sucked the water away. It was a slow, unpleasant job, and we usually took turns during the process because our hands got so cold.

The Shuttle does not have a food freezer, but the Space Station will have a refrigerator as well as a freezer. They will work like home appliances and have an automatic defrost feature. Incidentally, getting rid of frost accumulation can be a real challenge in weightlessness. When you defrost a refrigerator or freezer on Earth the frost is melted by heat and it collects in the bottom or drains into a pan where it evaporates. This doesn't happen in zero g so a method has to be provided to remove the melted frost. On Skylab we didn't have a way of melting the frost so we used washcloths lightly wetted with hot water.

55. How did you cook your food?

We didn't have to cook our food because it was already cooked, but we did warm solid foods (like precooked meats and vegetables) in their metal containers by placing them in food-tray cavities that were warmed by electrical heating elements. Skylab had a hot water system, and coffee or tea could be prepared easily and quickly.

The Shuttle astronauts use convective ovens, which take about a half hour to warm their food. The Space Station will have microwave ovens to heat their food, so the warming time will be much less — a matter of minutes — and uses up less electrical power.

56. How do you keep food on your plate?

We didn't have plates. Our food came in cans and plastic bags that fitted into cavities in our food trays with enough friction to keep them from floating out. We used a fork and spoon to get the food from the containers and a knife and fork to cut the solid meats.

There was a thin plastic cover over most of the canned food. We cut a crisscross slit in the plastic and fished the food out with a spoon or fork. The natural "stickiness" (surface tension) of the food and the plastic cover held it in quite well. Occasionally, little bits of food or meat juice would float out as we took a bite. We would dab at it with a tissue as it floated above the table, and we got most of it. Unfortunately, we didn't get it all, and the droplets would usually float up, owing to airflow, and stick to the ceiling. Thick soups and ice cream tended to stick to the spoon, so you could eat them normally, as long as you didn't make any abrupt movements.

The system used by Shuttle astronauts is similar: Their food trays are portable and the crew usually attaches them to the top of their thighs while they eat. After the Space Station is fully assembled one section (habitation module) will have tray tables similar to *Skylab*. The trays will be plastic, similar to the Shuttle trays and will have metal imbedded in the tableware resting space so that magnets in the tableware handles will keep the utensils in place.

57. Did you have ketchup and mustard?

Yes. It was in little plastic sacks similar to the kind you use at a fast-food restaurant. We also had hot sauce, liquid pepper in restaurant-type squeeze bottles, and horseradish, which we mixed into a paste and spread on our meat. The liquid pepper was especially good and had a full, fresh flavor. We had salt water in a dispenser that looked like a hypodermic syringe with a plastic nozzle. We squirted the salt solution directly on our food.

The first *Skylab* crew had no condiments at all. The commander, Pete Conrad, really blasted the planners when he got back and raised such a fuss about the bland, yucky-tasting food that condiments were finally added. The second crew tried regular ground pepper and salt, but they didn't work too well. The salt and pepper floated around and caused a lot of sneezing. By the time we launched, the dietitian had worked out a good scheme for dispensing a wide selection of condiments. Pete Conrad really did us a great service by insisting on the addition of condiments.

Shuttle astronauts have a wide variety of single-serving pouches and may select from: salt (water solution), liquid pepper, ketchup, mustard, taco sauce, Tabasco sauce, and mayonnaise. Space Station crews will have similar choices but will also include favorite condiments of the astronauts from other countries.

58. Did you have recycled water?

No. *Skylab* carried a total of about 1,000 gallons of water for drinking and bathing. If *Skylab* had been designed for repeated visits over several years, then recycling of water would have been practical. The simplest recycling system is to recover the water from the spacecraft atmosphere. This water would come from exhaled air and moisture evaporated from the skin, i.e., sweat. We actually removed this water, but we didn't use it for anything. It was collected in a wastewater tank.

The Russian cosmonauts started recycling and using this water in their *Salyut* space station in the early 1970s. A more complete water-recycling scheme would also include reprocessing (recovery) of water from all body waste (urine and feces).

No water recycling is required for the Shuttle because of the short flights. The system would weigh more than the water recovered and would be uneconomical. The water recovery (recycling) system designed for the Space Station involves two levels of use. Water for drinking and preparing food and beverages may come from cabin air or the original water stores brought up by the Shuttle and resupplied on a regular schedule. Other water reclaimed from the cabin air and urine recycling is used for bathing and general hygiene. Water with unacceptable levels of contaminants is removed from the system.

If this sounds offensive, just remember that the Earth is a closed life (ecological) system. Something has to happen to all the water in animal life waste. It is recycled through our natural system through evaporation and subsequent rainfall, if you're lucky. Some of it isn't even recycled through the natural system if your city water comes from a river downstream of another city using the river as a sewage dump. On moon bases or on a mission to Mars and at a Mars base, water will be a precious resource. Recycling systems will be a necessity.

59. How did you drink? What did you drink? Did you have alcoholic beverages onboard?

A water dispenser similar to a water gun was used to take a drink by holding the nozzle, or point of the dispenser, in the mouth and squirting the water directly in. Beverages were prepared by forcing water from hot- or cold-water dispensers into a plastic container containing a mixture that was dissolved by the water—we usually shook it up to mix it. The plastic container squeezed up like an accordion and had a valve on the nozzle to keep the liquid from leaking out. To drink from these containers, we put the nozzle in our mouths, opened the valve with our teeth, and squeezed the bag to squirt the drinks into our mouths. The system worked quite well except for the air we swallowed while drinking.

Shuttle astronauts use a similar system. Their drink containers are better designed and they use straws to drink. They still have the problem of stomach gas (described in Question 60, following). Some think it may be owed to gases dissolved in the water used to make the drinks. Milk was introduced for use on the Shuttle in 1990. The bacteria in the milk is killed using a high-temperature sterilization technique developed by Utah State University. This gives the milk a long shelf life without refrigeration. Currently, no alcoholic beverages are permitted on U.S. space missions.

60. Did you have trouble swallowing?

No. We had no trouble swallowing, but there was one bad aspect of swallowing drinks from the plastic drink containers. I think it bothered me more than the others. When I drank from the plastic squeeze-drink bags, I tended to swallow a lot of air with the liquid. This caused an uncomfortable pressure in my stomach that normally would be relieved by burping or belching. But—in weightlessness—the contents of the stomach don't settle; they coat the stomach more or less uniformly. So if you burp, you stand a very good chance of regurgitating. The gas pressure in the stomach is unpleasant, but the consequences of burping are even worse. I think I only burped twice in eighty-four days. Once my exercise period had been scheduled right after breakfast and I had only been pedaling the bicycle a short time when I got this strong desire to burp. I fought it, but it happened anyway. I gritted my teeth, swallowed it, and kept right on pedaling.

61. How did you wash dishes?

Because we ate directly from plastic bags or cans, the only things that required cleaning were our tableware and food trays. These were wiped with tissues soaked with a mild disinfectant. The cans were crunched flat with a special food-can crusher and placed in a bag for disposal. We didn't throw anything into space. Shuttle crew members use a similar system.

62. What did you do with the trash?

Each crew member produces a half-cubic foot of trash per day. That's a volume roughly equal to a large grocery bag and most of it is

WHAT DID YOU DO WITH THE TRASH?

food packaging. *Skylab* had a large tank about the size of a one-car garage (2,000 cubic feet) that was used as a trash-disposal volume or Dumpster. We compacted our garbage as much as possible, placed it in a special bag, and forced it through a large tube into the special tank below the floor. The tube contained an airlock chamber to prevent loss of air when we opened the hatch to the tube. The assembly was call a *trash airlock* (TAL).

The lid on the trash airlock began to cause difficulties on the second *Skylab* mission. The hatch became more and more difficult to latch in the closed position. On our mission, the problem became worse, and we were very concerned, because it was essential to get rid of the biodegradable garbage and waste (food residue and urine bags). We finally worked out a system whereby Jerry Carr would load the trash bag in the bin of the trash airlock and I would float above, holding onto the ceiling. As he closed the hatch, I would pull myself down sharply and stomp on the hatch lid while Jerry closed the locking lever. It sounds like a barnyard procedure, but it worked.

All trash and waste collected on the Shuttle is returned to Earth, but they have a trash compactor to compress the volume to $\frac{1}{5}$ before

STS 35 Onboard View   Flown for the first time, the trash compaction and retention system onboard Columbia gets used by Astronaut Robert A. P. Parker, mission specialist.

storing it. The Space Station will also use a trash compactor to reduce the trash volume and store it for later return to the Earth. It will be returned in a large freight carrier called the *logistics module*, which is hauled up and down by the Shuttle. Some trash or waste will be placed aboard a Russian *Progress* freighter, which will totally disintegrate while reentering the Earth's atmosphere.

63. Why didn't you just dump it out into space? Wouldn't it just burn up during reentry?

Dumping trash out into space is irresponsible because it adds to the space debris (junk) already contaminating the region used by manned spacecraft and some satellites. Ejected trash can remain in orbit for a long time and there is a reasonable chance that it (dumped waste) will collide with the spacecraft on a later orbit.

WHEN CLOTHES GOT DIRTY, WE
THREW THEM AWAY

64. How did you wash your dirty clothes?

We didn't. When they got dirty, we threw them away with the other trash. All trash was put into the large waste compartment at the rear of the space station. (See Question 62.)

Shuttle astronauts return their clothing, which is cleaned for reuse. When funding becomes available the Space Station will have a washer for clothing and bath linen. A washing machine will save weight by reducing the quantity of clothing, towels, and washcloths required during resupply from Earth.

65. What kind of clothes or underwear did you wear?

We wore trousers, T-shirts, and jackets. The jackets had snap tabs at the bottom of the back that could be fastened to the trousers to keep them from crawling up our back. The trousers had several pouch pockets with zipper closures or flap covers held closed by Velcro. The zippers and flaps were useful to prevent things from floating out. However, if you had a lot of things in a pocket, you never knew what would come out first when you reached inside. Our underwear was commercially manufactured briefs and T-shirts.

Shuttle and Space Station astronauts have a wide range in their clothing selections: one-piece coveralls, shorts with T-shirts, jackets, etc. Most seem to prefer working in stocking feet on the Shuttle. Before flight, the astronauts select their flight clothing at the Flight Equipment Processing Facility located near the Johnson Spacecraft Center at Houston, Texas. This facility assembles the food, clothing, space suits, cameras, special instruments, calculators, tools, etc. that are needed for each flight.

66. Did you have space pajamas? How did you get dressed, put on your socks and shoes?

We slept in our underwear. After we "weighed" ourselves each morning, we slipped on the *Skylab* T-shirts and trousers, and then floated into our shoes, which were left attached to the floor during the night. Because it was difficult to bend forward, we pulled our legs up to put on our socks and tie our shoes.

67. What would happen if your glove came off your suit during a space walk?

This is very unlikely to happen. The gloves are attached with a double-locking mechanism and it is easy to check that they are on properly (similarly with the helmet). It requires a concentrated effort to unlock and remove the gloves and helmet. However, if a glove came off, all the air would leak out and the astronaut would die.

68. How did you keep from getting too hot or too cold on a space walk?

We wore water-cooled one-piece long johns, called a *LCG* (liquid cooled garment). Cool water was circulated through plastic tubing throughout this mesh garment to remove body heat. We could control the water-flow rate to regulate the temperature. The Shuttle and Space Station astronauts use an improved version called a *LCVG* (liquid cooling and ventilation garment). In addition to the liquid-cooling feature, the LCVG includes air ducts to provide ventilation to the arms and legs. The LCVG has enabled simplification of the suit design.

However, the early Shuttle suit did not circulate enough heat to the gloves and astronauts on space walks reported many cases of cold hands when they were in the dark too long. This problem has been corrected by adding heaters to the gloves.

69. Did you wear glasses?

Yes, I took two pairs with me. I'm farsighted and needed glasses to read small print and instrument displays. I didn't wear glasses in the space suit because we didn't have a good eyeglass retention system; wearing glasses for close work ruined my distant vision, which I needed when transferring equipment to the other crew member.

70. Are astronauts allowed to wear contact lenses?

Yes, they can safely use contact lenses in space. Astronauts desiring to use contact lenses during space missions are encouraged to start using them during training at least one month prior to launch, and are required to carry eyeglasses as a backup. NASA flight physicians recommend soft contact lenses for astronauts not requiring a correction for astigmatism, and the gas permeable types for those that do need an astigmatism correction.

Astronaut William R. Pogue in a Spacesuit.   Note the bulkiness of the suit and the thickness of the gloves. The large unit on the front of the suit is a pressure control unit (PCU) that regulates pressure in the suit and the flow of water through the Liquid-Cooled Garment underneath. (See Question 64.)

Sleeping on the *Skylab*   Scientist-Astronaut Owen K. Garriot, science pilot on second *Skylab* mission, sleeps in the standard *Skylab* sleeping bag. (See Question 71.)

71. Did you just float around when you slept?

No. One member of our crew tried this once, but it didn't work too well because he drifted around with the airflow and kept bumping into things. We slept in sleeping bags supported by a tubular metal frame that was strapped to the wall of our individual sleep compartments. We slipped into the sleeping bag feetfirst through the neck hole.

There were arm slits in the bag, so we could reach out. It had straps on the front and back that we could tighten to hold us in a steady, snug position, and there were extra sleeping bag wraps that could be zipped on for greater warmth. Airflow, light, and temperature could be controlled in each sleep compartment.

Shuttle astronauts also use sleeping bags, which they position throughout the Shuttle compartments. A few have found it more convenient to sleep while strapped in a seat on the flight deck (commander and pilot seats). Some have said they couldn't get to sleep in the mid-deck (lower deck) of the Shuttle because of the noise from cooling fans. On some Shuttle missions sleep compartments are installed in the mid-deck area. One of the Shuttle astronauts that had used both the sleeping bag and the sleep compartment commented that the quality of sleep was much better when using the compartment because it reduced the noise a lot. The fully assembled Space Station will have individual crew quarters in the habitation module.

72. How long did you sleep?

About six hours was all we needed because we weren't using a lot of physical energy performing our tasks in weightlessness. We all slept at the same time and got wake-up calls at 6:00 A.M. central standard time. Shuttle *Spacelab* astronauts work in two twelve-hour shifts, twelve hours on and twelve hours off. This allows around-the-clock manning of *Spacelab*, which is needed to complete their busy schedule of work. When a full crew (six) is aboard the Space Station astronauts will use this two-shift system.

73. Was the sleep restful, the same as on Earth?

Yes, but I think there is a difference. Tests made on *Skylab* (using a cap with sensors that fit against the head) showed that there is a change in the time you spend at the different levels of sleep. Some Shuttle crews have continued the study of sleep quality using an improved version of the cap. Many times the sleep was fitful because of work-related stress and other difficulties. Also, some astronauts have been bothered by a peculiar effect known as "head nod." During full relaxation in sleep, the head develops a nodding motion. This nodding motion is thought to occur as a result of blood pulsing through the large arteries in the neck. Occasionally astronauts have been awakened by nausea symptoms that they blamed on the head nod. Others have noticed the head nod, but did not feel any ill effects from it.

74. Did you snore? Did anyone snore on *Skylab*? Did snoring bother you or keep you awake?

No. As far as I know, no one snored on *Skylab*, so it didn't bother me or keep me awake. In weightlessness, the position of the soft palate in the upper throat doesn't change with the body position, which is probably the reason people aren't as likely to snore in space. Most snoring occurs when a person lies on his/her back, thus causing the soft palate to hang down and vibrate during breathing. However, some Shuttle astronauts have reported loud and resonant snoring, so it does happen.

75. Did you have to do exercises?

Yes. Since it doesn't take much physical effort to move around in space, an astronaut must exercise regularly to prevent the muscles from getting weak. We were given about one-and-a-half hours a day to exercise. I normally spent half an hour on the stationary bicycle, fifteen minutes using spring and pulley (reel-type) exercisers, and ten minutes walking on the treadmill. On our day off, we sometimes skipped all exercises except the treadmill. We usually listened to music, using a stereo headset, while we were exercising on the bicycle, to help pass the time.

One time I was playing a new tape from Joe Kerwin's selection and really pumping hard as the workload increased at the end of the workout. I was tiring fast and wondering if I would be able to finish when the overture from *William Tell* started. It really gave me a shot of energy and I finished with power to spare. I was really surprised how much the music affected my performance.

As the Russian missions increased in length (*Salyut* and *Mir* space stations), they refined their exercise programs based on their postflight evaluations of the physical condition of the cosmonauts. They maintain that it is essential to exercise twice daily for a one-hour period. The two cosmonauts that completed a 366-day mission in December 1988, exercised diligently and were reported to be as fit as cosmonauts completing earlier missions of shorter duration.

76. What happens to sweat?

We got a lot of sweat on our backs when we pedaled the bicycle. It didn't drop off like it does here on Earth. The sweat on the back collected in a large puddle. By the end of half an hour of exercise, the puddle was as large as a dinner plate and about a quarter of an inch deep. It sort of slithered around on our backs as we pedaled the bicycle. When we were done, we had to move very carefully to avoid slinging off a large glob of sweat. It could have stuck to the walls of the spacecraft or onto equipment and caused problems. We used an old towel to mop the sweat off our backs before bathing.

Exercise really builds up a laundry pile; we started out exercising in T-shirts but we didn't have enough for each day and one use was enough to ruin the shirt. Eventually, we exercised wearing only our shorts. Also, the air circulation wasn't adequate around the stationary bicycle so we used a portable fan to cool us during the heavy exercise.

77. How did you keep from floating around while exercising?

Our shoes locked into the pedals of the bicycle, but this didn't take care of the entire problem. We needed something to hold our bodies down because we tended to float off the seat and pushed ourselves up as soon as we started pedaling. A harness restraint for the shoulders and upper body had been provided but it didn't work too well. We finally took the seat off and held our heads against a makeshift pad mounted against the ceiling to balance the up-force caused by pushing down on the pedals. For the spring and pulley exercisers, we locked our shoes in the floor to hold us in position while we exercised. The treadmill had a harness that held us down against the walking surface. The harness included strong elastic sections that

STS-44 Onboard View   Astronaut Terence T. (Tom) Henricks (foreground), pilot, "rows" on the modified treadmill device used by crew members for biomedical tests and for exercising. Earlier the treadmill had experienced an anomaly that affected its ability to support the subjects in "running" mode. Astronaut Mario Runco Jr., mission specialist, his torso bearing sensors, awaits his turn on the treadmill.

pulled us down toward the surface with a force roughly equal to our Earth body weight.

The design of exercise restraints have been greatly improved since *Skylab*. The exercise programs on the Shuttle missions have been intermittent because of the short, work-filled flight schedules. From video of their flights the restraint system for the treadmill appears to be quite good.

A variety of exercise devices are available for the International Space Station, including an ergometer (stationary bicycle), a treadmill, rowing machines, and exercisers simulating cross-country skiing.

78. Isn't it (exercise) boring?

Yes, and NASA has been working to solve this problem. Several different types of video displays similar to those available with commercial exercise units are available for use on the Space Station. Some display graphics of roads, turns, and hills with the effort required matched to the display. I think any visual diversion would be very effective to reduce the boredom during exercise. I also think music helps, particularly music with a tempo matched to the exercise.

79. How did you go to the bathroom?

On *Skylab*, for the first time in space, we had a separate room for a toilet called the *waste management compartment*. A funnel-shaped device was used to collect the urine. Air was drawn through the funnel to make sure the urine was pulled into the collection bag inside the device and this bag was changed daily. A commode, or potty, was used for solid-waste collection. It was mounted on the wall (remember, there is no up or down in space) and was lined with a porous bag that was replaced after each use. Air was drawn through the bag to settle the waste.

The bag containing the solid waste was removed after each use and dried in a heat/vacuum chamber. All solid waste was dried, stored, and returned to Earth for medical analysis. Also, each day a small sample of urine was taken and frozen. It too was stored and brought back for analysis.

The toilet seat was made of a plastic-coated, stiff cushion material.

Space Shuttle Toilet   This Waste Management Compartment was the first unisex bathroom in space, designed to meet the needs of both male and female astronauts. (See Question 79.)

A seat belt had to be used to keep the user's bottom from floating off the seat. Proper use of the toilet was essential if one wanted to avoid losing friends. Because of their recessed plumbing, women have a special problem urinating hygienically in weightlessness. To solve this problem, NASA studied the issue in detail. This involved the photography of the urination function performed by a group of women

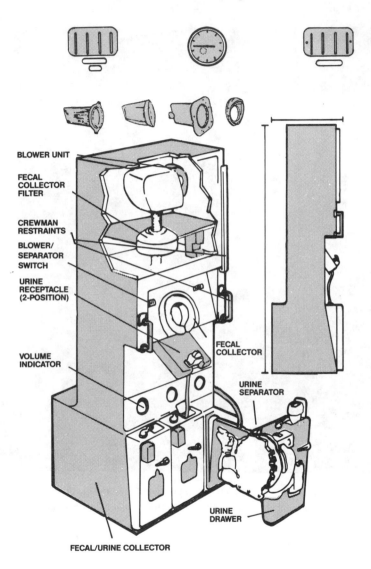

BLOWER UNIT

FECAL
COLLECTOR
FILTER

CREWMAN
RESTRAINTS

BLOWER/
SEPARATOR
SWITCH

URINE
RECEPTACLE
(2-POSITION)

VOLUME
INDICATOR

FECAL
COLLECTOR

URINE
SEPARATOR

URINE
DRAWER

FECAL/URINE COLLECTOR

volunteers. Based on their data, NASA developed a unisex toilet that is used on the Shuttle.

The unisex toilet consists of a potty seat similar to—but broader and flatter than—the *Skylab* commode, together with a urine-collection device located near the front of the toilet seat. The Shuttle toilet doesn't have a seat belt. Shuttle crew members are held down by two L-shaped thigh restraints that pull up from the sides of the commode. They are turned to place the bars on top of the thighs and, when released, springs pull the bar down on the top of the legs to hold the body on the commode seat.

In older spacecraft not furnished with a special toilet, the provisions were much cruder. Liquid waste was collected by the same method used on space walks. (See Question 81.) The urine was stored in a collection tank. Solid-waste collection was much more difficult. We used a fecal-collection bag, about eight inches across, with an adhesive ring surface around the top. The user stuck this bag to his bottom. After use, the solid waste was treated with chemical tablets to kill bacteria, and the bag was placed in a waste container.

This technique wasn't foolproof. Occasionally, fecal matter inadvertently floated free, unobserved by the user; and later drifted into view. Usually, no one would admit responsibility, and the event was cause for a lot of ribald comments. I can personally attest that fecal and urine spills can break the monotony on even the dullest days In space.

80. Have there been failures of the Shuttle toilet?

Yes, there have been failures in the original Shuttle solid-waste and the urine-waste collection systems. When the solid-waste collection system fails, the astronauts resort to using Apollo-type fecal-collection bags. (See Question 79.) Each Shuttle mission carries two bags per day per crew member, with enough for a two-day mission extension. For backup urine collection the crew can use commercial adult diapers, which are very effective in absorbing the urine and protecting the skin from continued contact with moisture. For Shuttle mission STS-54 an improved waste-collection system (IWCS) was installed for better hygiene and to increase capacity; it is also much more reliable. The commode seat is similar to the one used on *Skylab*. The IWCS does not have to be removed for servicing between flights, which reduces the work by Shuttle ground crews. The toilets for the Space Station are similar to the IWCS design.

81. How did you go to the bathroom on a space walk?

We had two devices to wear under our space suits. A UCD (urine collection device) for urine, and a FCS (fecal containment system) for solid waste. The UCD was attached to an undergarment with Velcro and connected to the body by a rubber sleeve containing a check valve to prevent urine from leaking back out of the bag.

The FCS was a tight-fitting, thigh-length trunk made of thick fabric. If required, the astronaut would defecate directly into the FCS. I know of no one who ever used this system, but it was good that we had it available, because we spent several hours out on space walks during *Skylab*. When we returned from space walks, we removed the waste-collection devices and transferred the contents to the appropriate containers.

Shuttle and Space Station astronauts have several options for urine collection on space walks. Male crew members may use the UCD or the commercial adult diapers used by women. The adult diaper is lined with a one-way transmission layer that conducts the urine to a superabsorbent material that is capable of holding over a quart of liquid. For launch and entry, the same options for urine collection are employed.

82. How did you bathe?

We had to bathe just about every day because we got very sweaty during exercise. On workdays, we took a sponge bath, using a washcloth, soap, and water; on our days off—once a week—we had about a half a gallon (two liters) of warm water for a shower.

To take a sponge bath, we started by gently squirting water on a washcloth from the water dispenser in the bathroom. The water stuck to the washcloth and looked like a thick layer of gelatin; we had to move it carefully over to our bodies. As the water touched the body, it would stick and spread over an area a bit larger than the washcloth. The entire body was wetted this way, then lathered with soap. Then as much soap lather as possible was removed with the washcloth, which could be wrung out in a special cloth squeezer. Next, water was again spread on the body and again mopped up, until the soap was removed. A towel was then used to dry. It took about thirty minutes to take a sponge bath.

A shower also took a long time — about half an hour. We had a zero-gravity shower stall, which was a circular sleeve — about three feet in diameter — with a stationary bottom attached to the floor and a circular top mounted on the ceiling. The sleeve's wall surface was fastened to the top when ready to shower and fully enclosed the user. Once inside the shower stall, a spray nozzle was used to squirt water on the body and a vacuum-cleaner attachment was used to suck off the soapy water both from the skin and from the walls of the shower stall. It was important to save enough water for rinsing off the soap. One *Skylab* crew member refused to use it at all.

I really did not enjoy the shower. It took a lot of work to get the equipment set up and I got chilled after the shower. The air was so dry that when I opened the shower stall, the rapid evaporation caused uncontrollable shivering for about a minute.

The Shuttle doesn't have a shower, so the astronauts take sponge baths. The fully assembled Space Station is designed to have two showers available and the objective is to make it much easier to use than the *Skylab* shower.

83. When you didn't bathe did you stink?

Yes, and it's not very pleasant. One day I was running short on time and skipped washing my hair after exercise. About two hours later I was operating the solar telescopes and began noticing an unpleasant odor. I thought it was food residue. Ed Gibson frequently snacked during his tour at the telescopes so I looked around for old food packages but couldn't find anything that might have caused the odor. The odor persisted and soon it became obvious that it was my own body odor. It was clinging around my head like a cocoon of smelly air. There is no convection in weightlessness (warm air around the body doesn't rise). There wasn't good air circulation in this location so I was being enveloped by my own body odor.

84. How did you shave?

We had commercial twin-blade razors, brushless shaving cream in a tube, and also a windup rotary mechanical razor. I tried the windup razor but found it to be very poor. It pulled the whiskers as much as it cut them off. I shaved with the blade razors for about two weeks, then stopped shaving and grew a beard. The blade razors were only good for one smooth shave, probably because there was no good way to rinse the shaving cream and whiskers from under the blades. We wiped the razor off on a washcloth by squirting water on it and wringing the cloth in a washcloth wringer. It took about fifteen minutes to shave. When I stopped shaving, it freed up some valuable early-morning time.

Shuttle and Space Station astronauts may use electric or blade razors. For blade razors they have a choice of three types of commercial shaving cream.

85. Did you age less on your space journey? How much?

According to the theory of relativity, time flows at different rates under different conditions. Time passes more slowly: (1) for a person in a higher gravitational field than he normally experiences; (2) if the person is under accelerated motion; or (3) if the person is traveling at a very high speed—near the speed of light.

An astronaut experiences some of these effects, although to a very slight degree. In orbit, an astronaut is under a *weaker* gravitational pull than at the surface of the Earth; this speeds up time, and therefore aging. But an astronaut experiences accelerated motion during launch and reentry, which slows down time and aging. In orbit an astronaut is traveling at about five miles per second, which is far too low to cause a relativistic decrease in the aging rate. I don't know what the final result is because the changes are too small to be determined by the spacecraft instruments.

86. Can you hear as well in space?

We had difficulty hearing each other beyond twenty-five feet. Part of this was owed to the noise level in *Skylab*, but some of it was

WE HAD DIFFICULTY HEARING
EACH OTHER

probably caused by the thin air, as the atmosphere was about one-third as dense as air on the Earth's surface. There was no detectable change in the ear's ability to hear.

The Shuttle's cabin pressure is about the same as on the Earth's surface and the compartments are smaller. Any difficulty in hearing each other is probably owed to the high noise level. (See Question 45.)

87. Did you have trouble talking? Did your voice change at all?

No, we didn't have any difficulty talking, even though the air was much thinner than air on Earth. We did not notice any change in voice pitch like the "Donald Duck" effect that deep-sea divers notice from breathing a thin or low density gas such as helium.

However, Shuttle tests with voice-activated devices indicate that there are changes in voice quality. Astronaut test subjects' voices changed enough to require "retraining" the device used to respond to voice commands. Voice-activated equipment will permit astronauts to control equipment with simple word commands when they have both hands busy with a task. This is especially helpful during space walks if they use equipment designed to respond to voice commands.

88. Do things taste and smell the same?

There do appear to be some slight changes in the sense of taste, smell, appetite, and food preference. I didn't think the taste or flavors were as strong as on Earth. Part of this may have been caused by the head stuffiness or nasal congestion I had. On our flight, we repeated taste and odor tests that we had done on Earth before the flight. The results were different for each person, and no consistent patterns were determined. There does seem to be an increase in the use of condiments. Astronauts who normally avoid hot and spicy foods have been observed to use Tabasco sauce quite liberally after a few days in space.

89. How did you tell time in space?

There is no "natural" time zone for space. However, it is important to use a single time standard so that mission planners and investigators from different countries can avoid confusion when scheduling activities. This standard is referred to as *GMT* (Greenwich mean time), the time at Greenwich, England. If you wish to include the date and year as well, then the time is referred to as *UT* (universal time).

To tell time during the mission we wore commercial wristwatches and also had several electronic clocks in the spacecraft. Our daily routine (work/sleep times) was based on central time in the United States. Our wake-up call came at 6:00 A.M. U.S. central standard time (CST). Of course, day and night periods in orbit changed much faster than on Earth (sixteen sunrises and sunsets every twenty-four-hour Earth day). I wore a wristwatch on each arm, with one set on GMT and one set on CST. All the *Skylab* clocks displayed GMT. Experiments and work tasks were scheduled on GMT. However, the work shifts at mission control and our meals were scheduled on the CST cycle; it was helpful to have both times available.

For shorter missions like Apollo and the Shuttle, mission elapsed time (MET) may be used. MET is useful when it is important to schedule events from liftoff (launch) time. If the liftoff time changes owing to a delay, the MET schedule (flight plan timeline), based on the actual liftoff time, will still be usable. For example, an event scheduled for MET 2:16 would be two hours and sixteen minutes after liftoff. During our mission, daylight saving time was instituted as a fuel-saving move during the oil shortage of the early 1970s. After that we used central daylight time (CDT) instead of CST.

90. How can you tell up from down?

In weightlessness, there is no up or down insofar as your body feel is concerned. However, we did prefer moving to a position so that things "looked" right-side-up to the eyes. It was amusing to watch one of the other crewmen looking out the window toward Earth. He would always move his head or body around until his head was "up" facing the horizon.

It is also better to use a common "up/down" (architectural) positioning of work stations in a given area. A common orientation of control and display panels helps prevent mistakes in display interpretation or in operating switches and controls.

91. Does it make you dizzy when you do tumbling and acrobatics?

Yes, in a way. Doing rapid rotations or tumbling gives you a strong, giddy, dizzy feeling like you get on a ride at an amusement park. The strange thing about it is that the dizziness isn't disorienting or the

THERE IS NO UP OR DOWN

least bit nauseating after the first few days in space. It's a fairly powerful sensation with no ill effects.

92. What is a space suit made of?

The Apollo and *Skylab* suits were similar and had about fifteen layers of material. Starting from the inside, the suit contained the following materials:

Having fun in Zero Gravity   Astronaut William R. Pogue (bottom) gives Scientist-Astronaut Jerry Carr a lift in weightlessness during the third *Skylab* Mission in 1974.

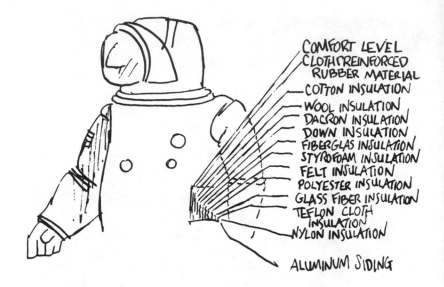

COMFORT LEVEL
CLOTH-REINFORCED
   RUBBER MATERIAL
COTTON INSULATION
WOOL INSULATION
DACRON INSULATION
DOWN INSULATION
FIBERGLAS INSULATION
STYROFOAM INSULATION
FELT INSULATION
POLYESTER INSULATION
GLASS FIBER INSULATION
TEFLON CLOTH
   INSULATION
NYLON INSULATION
ALUMINUM SIDING

A SPACESUIT MAY HAVE 15 LAYERS

1. A soft comfort layer of heat-resistant material called *Nomex*.
2. A gastight bladder of cloth-reinforced rubberlike material, neoprene-coated nylon.
3. Many layers of insulating materials.
4. A protective outer layer of glass fiber and Teflon cloth to protect against small meteoroids and fire.

The bubble helmet was formed of a high-strength plastic called *Lexan*. Altogether the suit weighed about forty pounds. These suits were customized (tailor-made), expensive, and had a limited service life.

For the Shuttle a new suit was designed so it would be less expensive, enable "off-the-rack" fitting for a crew member, and would last a lot longer (fifteen-year service life with proper maintenance). It is referred to as the *EMU* (extravehicular mobility unit) and consists of three major components: the upper torso (also referred to as the *HUT* or hard upper torso), the lower torso (or trousers), and the portable life-support system (PLSS, pronounced *pliss*). The HUT is constructed of aluminum and the "trousers" are similar to earlier suits. The PLSS is permanently mounted to the HUT, with all connections internally attached. This eliminates the external hoses and water connections that were required on the earlier lunar-surface suits. The lower and upper parts are joined together at a waist ring.

The Shuttle suit does not have to be connected to the spacecraft with a hose (umbilical). It is similar in appearance to the suit used by the Apollo astronauts on the moon but has many improvements and has enough oxygen and electrical power for seven hours of operation. The Shuttle suit will be used on the Space Station until a new suit is available.

93. What do astronauts do for entertainment?

On *Skylab* we had an entertainment kit that included books, playing cards, squeeze-type hand exercisers, some balls, a Velcro-covered dartboard with Velcro-tipped darts, three stereo tape players with headsets and cabinet speakers, and a pair of binoculars. We each selected our own music tapes and books in advance of our mission, and these were stowed onboard *Skylab* prior to its launch (unmanned).

We used the tape players, binoculars, and books more than any of the other items. The darts didn't work too well. Their fins were small, and because of the thin atmosphere in *Skylab* (one-third the atmospheric pressure of Earth), they wobbled around when they were thrown. The second *Skylab* crew tried enlarging the fins, but it didn't help much.

Sometimes entertainment opportunities came up quite unexpectedly. We had dry-roasted peanuts in small cans with thin plastic covers. The covers had crisscross cuts to allow us to reach in with our fingers to pull out the peanuts. Occasionally, a peanut would float out of its container, and as we made our way through the Space Station, we would notice it drifting and tumbling through the air. When this happened, we would get against the wall, open our mouths wide, shove off toward the peanut, and try to capture it with our mouths like a fish. Sometimes we were lucky enough to catch it on the first attempt, but usually we would bump it, which would send it twirling off away from us.

I found that looking at the Earth with the binoculars was the most pleasant form of off-duty activity. The Earth was fascinating, and I never tired of looking at it. Next to this, I enjoyed the books and music the most. Floating acrobatics were also a lot of fun.

Shuttle astronauts have carried a variety of devices and improvised with onboard equipment to play mock games of soccer, football, golf, and basketball. Astronauts on the Space Station will have video players that will support a wide variety of recreational video activities. In addition to movies, two-way family communications, etc., they are capable of supporting electronic games. Cosmonauts have had two-way video capability for several years.

94. Could you play basketball in space?

We didn't, but Shuttle astronauts have played a sort of basketball game with a miniature hoop and a six-inch ball. Of course, they don't play basketball in the normal way, and getting the ball to bounce through the hoop requires a little practice. I haven't seen any of them dribbling the ball, though. That would be a bit of a real challenge.

Controlling a bouncing ball in weightlessness is tough. On *Skylab* we had three small balls in the recreation kit, and we played with them occasionally. When we threw them around, they bounced all over the place because of weightlessness. The hardest part was trying to find the ball when you were done. It's sort of like playing three-dimensional billiards.

95. What was it like on the rocket going up?

When the engines fire up, they sound like muffled explosions, and there are a lot of noises from engine pumps and liquid fuel (propellants) surging through the large pipes (feed lines). Early in the launch, there is a lot of shaking and vibration. As the rocket picks up speed, it lurches, twitches, and wiggles from thrust pulsations and abrupt swiveling (gimballing) of the engines to steer the rocket. It feels like being on top of a skinny hotdog that's being shoved through the sky.

THEY BOUNCED ALL OVER THE PLACE

There is a lot of swishing air noise as the rocket picks up speed. After the speed becomes supersonic, the swishing air noise suddenly stops, and then you can hear the noises from deep within the rocket, mostly creaks and groans. When the fuel is burned out of the first stage, it is discarded or cut loose by explosives (pyrotechnics). This is really an experience—it sounds like a train wreck. There are banging noises and flashes from the explosives and from the little rocket engines that pull the spent stage away from the tail of the next stage. You can also see a lot of metal pieces flying away and twirling lazily around the rocket. Staging only takes a few seconds, but it seems much longer. Then the engine of the next stage fires, and you're off toward orbit.

Shuttle astronauts give a similar dramatic account of their launches and all first-time space travelers comment on the excitement of the ride. As long as we launch crews with rockets I think it will be an exciting experience. Perhaps when we develop an aerospace plane—one that can take off from a runway and fly into orbit—it won't be quite as dramatic.

96. Were you ever really scared?

One of the NASA doctors asked me if I were scared at liftoff. I told him I didn't feel particularly excited. He said, "Well, that may be true, but your heart rate went from forty-eight to one-twenty at liftoff." I still don't think I was scared, but I must have been excited.

An old cliché often quoted by pilots is that "flying consists of hours and hours of boredom interrupted occasionally by moments of stark terror." I've also heard test pilots and astronauts say that they don't experience fear, merely varying levels of anxiety or apprehension. I think some of them are telling the truth, but I also think they are expressing a distinction between fear and panic. A person can be genuinely afraid but, through discipline, self-control, training, experience, and professional competence, can still function rationally and effectively to cope with problems or emergencies.

It is also true that a person can become conditioned to react with some degree of detachment when faced with serious and life-threatening situations, particularly when they occur within the individual's area of professional expertise. If anyone can claim such self-control, I think it would be experimental test pilots, particularly those that are still around to talk about it. However, I believe anyone is capable of experiencing fear—and a high level of concern for personal safety, prestige, or professional status. The key is to avoid panic at all costs, and this is best achieved by being well-trained. Also, I don't equate excitement with fear. A bit of controlled excitement really gets the mind alert and working.

All three of us got a real shock just after we had jettisoned our service module after the deorbit thrusting maneuver. The attitude required for this jettison task was way off the attitude required for reentry, which was only minutes away. At this point Jerry was to maneuver to the entry attitude using the attitude control rockets on the reentry module (command module). When nothing happened I looked over and saw him moving the controller but it was obvious the jets weren't firing in response to the command. I yelled "go direct!" (a backup method), but he had already switched over and the thrusters fired. That was the sweetest noise I'd heard in three months. We were already a bit concerned because one of the two attitude rocket systems had already failed and had been turned off. During that brief period I would say that I was scared. If we hadn't been able to get to the right attitude with the heat shield facing forward for reentry, it would have gotten very warm inside.

97. What is the greatest fear in space?

The greatest concerns are fire, loss of air from the spacecraft, and contamination of the internal spacecraft atmosphere (breathing air). We had fire extinguishers on *Skylab*, and we also had emergency procedures to follow in the event of fire or rapid loss of pressure. Atmosphere contamination was not a great concern to us on *Skylab* because there were no sources of contamination (other than caused by fire).

However, some Shuttle/*Spacelab* missions and the Space Station carry chemicals for materials processing and biological experiments. Accidental releases of these materials could possibly contaminate the atmosphere but it's not a great risk. Leaks on Spacelab missions have occurred but have posed no serious threat to the crew.

The Space Station will use a number of different materials that could contaminate the atmosphere inside the station. However, these are all contained within barriers that prevent their release. For really nasty materials the Space Station has three barriers to provide protection (triple containment). All spacecraft have caution and warning systems to signal alarms and inform the crew of the nature of the problem. The audio alarms are unmistakable and really get your attention.

One day the fire alarm sounded as I was exercising on the bicycle.

It was a blood-chilling sound, and I never liked to hear it, even when we were testing the alarm system. It turned out to be a false alarm, but it took me about half an hour to check out everything and determine that it *was* a false alarm. Our fire sensors detected ultraviolet (uv) light (emitted by fire). However, sunlight contains ultraviolet light and the false alarm was probably owed to reflections of sunlight that came through a window in our wardroom. The window filtered out most of the uv but enough passed through to activate the alarm sensor. When the alarm had sounded my back was covered with sweat from the heavy exercise. I leaped off the bicycle so fast I slung off several large globs of sweat that splashed and bounced on a wall nearby. After checking out the alarm I had to mop up the mess with a towel.

98. How do you know when the spacecraft is perfect for launch? What is the risk of going into space?

There is no such thing as a perfect spacecraft or booster rocket. All equipment that is launched has flaws or imperfections. Some of these are known to exist and other problems don't appear until during the launch or after the spacecraft is in space. The people who prepare the hardware for launch must consider all the known problems and decide which are safety-critical—that is, which problems may be a significant risk to crew safety or prevent accomplishing the main jobs scheduled for the mission. Problems that are considered critical must be corrected before launch. Other problems that are minor or merely nuisance imperfections may not be corrected.

Undetected problems or problems that arise during the mission are handled various ways. Things (functions) that are critical are duplicated within the design of the spacecraft so if one system or thing fails there is another independent system to provide that same function. For instance, the Shuttle has five independent computers to perform the calculations required during launch and reentry. If one fails there are four others left to do the job. Another way to correct for a failure during the mission is to repair the problem.

Other risks or hazards of space flight may be caused by human failures. People may make a bad decision or may make a mistake in performing their job. The *Challenger* disaster was caused by a bad decision. This cost the lives of seven astronauts. I made many mistakes during the three-month *Skylab* mission. Sometimes they were minor and merely required repeating the job. On other occasions the mistake caused the loss of film or data.

The space program uses many ways to try to avoid human errors such as using one group to check the work of another group. These checks and verifications are usually very effective in identifying problems. In the case of the *Challenger* explosion this system failed to operate effectively. Basically, NASA and industry people were under a lot of pressure to meet launch schedules with insufficient resources to do the job. They failed to keep safety considerations as the number-one priority and made a decision to go ahead with the launch even though good judgment would have dictated otherwise.

Many changes have been made in the NASA management system in order to assure that groups concerned with safety have a strong voice in making decisions when any question arises. However, there is absolutely no way to guarantee that space accidents will not happen again; it simply isn't possible. It is possible to enforce a system to reduce the probability of another space failure and this is what NASA has done. There will always be an element of risk in any space flight.

99. What kind of problems did you launch with?

Two days before our scheduled launch an inspector discovered cracks in all eight tail fins of our Saturn rocket booster. This was considered a serious problem and the launch was delayed a week while the fins were replaced. After the fin replacement another inspection revealed cracks in the interstage trusses that connected the two stages of the booster rocket. These flaws were called "stress corrosion cracks" and could only be seen with a magnifying glass. A meeting was held to consider the risk and it was decided that these latest cracks did not pose a hazard.

Our launch had already been delayed a week for the fin replacement and when we were told about the stress corrosion cracks I remarked to Jerry Carr that we ought to name our booster rocket "Humpty Dumpty" because they were finding so many cracks in it. Later, Jerry casually mentioned our proposed name to the launchpad manager who had been working around-the-clock supervising the repair work crews who had accomplished the fin replacement and inspection work. He didn't appear to find the remark amusing.

The next morning we were atop the rocket in our spacecraft waiting for launch. In between the many checks we were confirming with the launch director, he would read "good luck" messages from the different teams that had participated in our training and launch preparation. It was rather nice and helped pass the time. Finally, the launch director said, "I have one final message," and Jerry Carr said, "Go ahead." The launch director read it slowly: "To the crew of *Skylab* Four, Good Luck and Godspeed—signed: All the King's horses and all the King's men." We had a good laugh and thanked the repair team for all their hard work. It somehow seemed reassuring to know they had a good sense of humor. Although we didn't launch with bad fins we did have minor problems with the computer display that we were all aware of and launched with that problem.

100. Did you get homesick?

I didn't get homesick in the strictest sense, that is, I didn't fret about it. We all missed familiar faces, but it wasn't a real psychological or emotional problem because we were so busy. We were also mentally prepared to stay in space for eighty-four days; that was our goal, and we were psychologically oriented to the eighty-four day mission.

There was also an interesting personal reaction I observed in myself as we neared the end of the eighty-four day mission. There was some consideration of extending our mission for two more weeks. We didn't hear too much about it onboard, but we were unanimously opposed when some veiled suggestions were made. We quickly pointed out that we were out of food, which was technically correct. However, we probably could have scraped together enough spare meals from leftover food items to last two weeks. I remember thinking that extending the mission was a lousy idea. I had stayed up for the agreed-upon time, and that was that. In retrospect, I think my reaction would have been different if the approach had been different and had been made by the right person or if some emergency or operational problem

WE COULD HAVE SCRAPED TOGETHER
ENOUGH SPARE MEALS

had required it. We all missed being around people, particularly family and friends. When we got back, it was very satisfying just to have a lot of different faces around.

There is an ongoing study of the problem of long-term isolation and confinement. The Russians have much more space experience with this issue than we do and appear to have a lot of data based upon professional observation/evaluation of their cosmonauts during and after their missions. Analysis of the experience gleaned from Antarctic "winter-over" teams, and nuclear-powered submarine crews has provided many valuable insights into the problem of isolation and confinement. This becomes a critical mission-planning issue when considering a manned flight to Mars. A Mars mission will last from 2½–3 years, much of which is spent in transit (outbound and return legs).

101. What was the hardest thing to get used to?

The head congestion or stuffiness. This was a minor problem on most space flights, but I seemed to have it a bit worse than my two fellow crew members. In space the sinuses don't drain as readily as they do on Earth; there's no postnasal drip in space.

102. Didn't you get bored on such a long mission of eighty-four days?

We were kept very busy, so boredom wasn't a problem. Many of the experiments we operated required a lot of operator input and the creative involvement led to a high level of individual job satisfaction. I believe this was a key factor in preventing boredom. If your tasks are all strictly mechanical, only following inflexible procedures, then you very quickly lose interest or question your value in the effort.

I would have really enjoyed having more time to relax and look out the window. The U.S. experience with this problem doesn't even come close to the wealth of data the cosmonauts have provided. From informal reports, it appears that they do have a problem with personal motivation during their long missions. Russian observers have commented on the progressive decrease in the time the cosmonauts can tolerate operating experiments during their work days.

103. Was it possible to get any privacy?

Yes, we each had a separate sleep compartment with a fabric door and we would use this to read as well as sleep. Also, *Skylab* was quite large, so it was possible to get privacy by going to another part of the space station. One rather amusing aspect of our sleep compartments was caused by the Velcro strips that latched our doors. The doors were really fabric sheets. When one of us got up at night to go to the bathroom, we opened the door by pushing open the Velcro strip. It sounded like someone was ripping open a shipping crate, and it frequently awakened the others. One night Jerry woke me, so I got up to look out the window for a few minutes. He was already there; we were over the Pacific Ocean somewhere and finally figured out we were flying over the Society Islands. We saw Tahiti, but it was mostly under clouds. After watching the coast of Chile come up, we gave it up and went back to bed.

The fully assembled International Space Station will have individual crew quarters to provide privacy. A cosmonaut visiting the Johnson Space Center was shown a mock-up (model) of these crew quarters and expressed alarm when he saw that the quarters could be closed off with sliding doors. He expressed the view that crew members shouldn't be allowed to shut themselves off from the others.

Perhaps it's a difference in the social or cultural habits, or it may be that we have something to learn when we begin staying up for longer periods.

104. How did your crew get along together?

Just fine. We were usually very busy, and there were so many problems with equipment that we had to help each other often. We had a good team spirit.

The only time the team spirit broke down was when I tried to draw a blood sample from Dr. Gibson. We had to do this every two weeks; Ed Gibson would draw Jerry's sample, Jerry would draw mine, and I was supposed to take one from Ed. Ed's veins were very small and I was probably the most inept at performing this task. After trying about ten times and causing Ed a lot of grief, he took the syringe away from me and drew his own sample. After that he never came back to me; he had Jerry do it, and it was never mentioned again.

105. Did you ever get mad at each other or have fights or arguments?

We didn't have any fights, and there was only one argument that I can recall. It had to do with a change in procedure, and the instructions were very vague. We resolved this by trying the procedure to see if it worked. We never got truly angry at each other, but we were frequently upset with or had disagreements with some people in mission control. We were all trying hard to get a job done, so there was probably fault on both sides at one time or another.

I think I upset Ed Gibson one day by putting his ice cream in the food warmer and leaving his steak in the freezer. I really felt badly about it. He couldn't eat the steak because it was still frozen hard, and the ice cream had turned to milk. He had to dig out some leftover food to make a meal. There wasn't too much conversation at dinner that night. He salvaged the ice cream by refreezing it. While the ice cream was in liquid form it turned into a big hollow ball. The next day, after it refroze, he stuffed it full of freeze-dried strawberries and had the first strawberry sundae in space.

106. Are you still friends?

Yes. Jerry Carr and I have worked together on several projects related to the Space Station and several advanced studies and projects. I see Ed Gibson about once a year.

107. What would you do if another guy went crazy?

This is not a silly question, and the astronaut selection process includes psychological evaluation. Isolation and confinement can cause severe mental stress in some people, and it's difficult to predict to whom it will occur and also the extent of irrational behavior. Our crew had talked with an individual who had witnessed one such derangement in an Arctic situation, and he gave us a good idea of the warning signs.

There are a lot of symptoms well before the time a person might cause harm to himself or others. The first sign is surliness and a general tendency to be uncooperative; the next is withdrawal from others. After a period of reclusiveness, the person gradually becomes openly antagonistic and aggressive toward others. If I were to have this problem, I would expect the other crew members to use whatever means available—be it medication or physical force—to control me while preparing to make an emergency/precautionary de-orbit and return to Earth.

WHAT IF ANOTHER GUY
WENT CRAZY?

For a long mission like a journey to Mars, it will not be possible to perform a quick return to Earth. Handling a mental derangement problem will be one of the issues requiring careful advanced planning for such missions.

108. What would you do if someone died?

As missions become longer and more and more people go into space, the natural death of a crew member in space becomes inevitable. For the Space Station, the plan is to store the body in a respectful fashion and return the deceased on the next Shuttle flight. It has not yet (as of 1999) been determined exactly how the body will be stored while awaiting return.

One proposed procedure would be to place the deceased in a suit or body bag and place him outside in an area permanently shaded from the sun. The cold temperature would preserve the body.

The use of a suit does not seems realistic to me. It would be no better than a body bag and a needless use of a suit that might be needed for an operational emergency. Another proposal is to place him in a freezer in the galley area. This doesn't appear practical to me. It would take up most of the freezer space and the immediate presence of the body would almost certainly have a depressing effect on the astronauts' morale.

Burial in space, similar to burial at sea, is considered unacceptable in Earth orbit. First, because there would be a need to do an autopsy, and second, because the body would remain in orbit and pose a safety hazard. However, this may be the only option on a long interplanetary mission. The disposition of deceased astronauts on Mars missions or on the moon has not been considered, although conventional burial on the moon or Mars appears to be feasible.

109. Did anyone get sick and vomit?

Yes. I threw up the first day of the flight. This was an unpleasant surprise because, according to tests we took while preparing for our mission, I was the least likely one of our crew to get sick. I used a burp bag similar to those available on airlines. About half of the astronauts feel sick the first few days in space, but after about three days this is no longer a problem.

110. Did anyone get ill enough to need medical care? Were you prepared to take care of medical problems?

None of us had a serious medical condition. The worst problems we had were skin irritations, bloodshot eyes, headaches, head congestion, and cuts from working on equipment in hard-to-reach areas. We had been given limited medical training, including the ability to treat broken bones and sew up cuts. Also, we could talk to doctors on Earth to get advice. We could have even shown the doctors the problems by using television that we could send down to Earth.

We could cope with nonserious problems, but in the case of serious injury or illness, we would have given the person emergency treatment and returned to Earth. For example, if a person had an appendicitis attack, we would have given antibiotics to control infection and brought him back at the first good opportunity. We had a heart needle and a tracheotome to treat urgent emergencies like cardiac arrest and throat blockage. NASA provided a small pharmacy that included decongestants for stuffiness, sleeping pills, motion sickness pills, antibiotics for internal infection, and aspirin for headaches. For Shuttle missions usually one or more of the mission specialists have received paramedic-type training and many have qualified physicians on the crew. Similarly, for the Space Station, they will have a physician on the crew (or someone with paramedic skills). For a Mars mission, it will be essential to have at least one physician with a backup (physician or paramedic); someone with dental training will also be needed. Within the astronaut group there are many qualified physicians.

111. How did you know what medicine to use?

We used our own experience for minor things such as headaches and stuffy heads. We did have to report any medications taken. For more complicated illnesses, we would have referred to our medical treatment book or consulted with the doctors on Earth.

112. What would you do if someone got a toothache?

First, we would have treated it with medication. If that didn't work, we had all the equipment and training necessary to remove the tooth. We weren't trained to fill teeth.

113. If you cut yourself, would you bleed?

Yes, you would, but the blood wouldn't drop off. It would collect in a ball over the cut. If there was enough blood, it would just spread out on your skin. We had tissues and bandages to clean and dress any wounds.

114. Did your position of sleeping—up or down—affect the fluid shift?

No. There is no up or down in weightlessness as far as the body is concerned. The fluid shift we experienced was caused by muscle tension in the legs, which caused certain body fluids to move toward the head and upper body. It had nothing to do with our position.

115. What happens when you sneeze? Would it propel you backwards?

This is an intriguing question. I didn't have that experience—that is, sneezing when I was floating freely and able to respond to the sneeze. The air rushes out your nose at about 100 miles per hour during a sneeze so it would act like a small jet or rocket and would propel you upward and rotate you backward. It would be somewhat like what happens when you let go of a balloon when the neck isn't plugged. But because the body is so much heavier, the motion wouldn't be nearly as great as the balloon. The body motion resulting from a sneeze would, most likely, be less than the effect caused by the spacecraft-cabin air circulating against your body.

However, I performed a simple calculation based on my body size and the result was that a sneeze would cause me to do a complete backward somersault in about twenty minutes and move me about five feet upward during the somersault. Of course, that's neglecting the effect of normal cabin air circulation.

View From Space: Northeastern U.S. and Atlantic Coastline Long Island can be clearly seen as the spit of land jutting out of the right. The Hudson River appears as a dark band extending towards the upper left of the picture. To the lower left are the Appalachian Mountains. (See Question 116.)

116. What could you see? What Earth features show up best?

Most of the time we saw oceans and clouds, but on almost every orbit we were able to get a good view of some land areas. The Earth features easiest to identify were coastlines, large lakes and rivers, major mountain ranges, and desert regions. Often it was like looking at a map, particularly when looking straight down at cloud-free land surfaces.

When we looked straight down toward the Earth, we could see a distinctive feature as small as a football field. Color or shading contrast and unusual shapes were particularly helpful in improving our ability to detect and identify features. We were able to see icebergs about a hundred yards in diameter quite easily because of the contrast of white ice with the dark-blue sea.

When we looked at pieces of hardware in space, we were able to see them with much greater clarity because of the absence of air. We noticed this first during launch, when our escape rocket and spacecraft cover were jettisoned about fifty miles above the Earth. As the rocket engines pulled the cover off the front and away from our spacecraft, we were able to see an unusual amount of detail in the structure of the cover. It seemed as though we could see every rivet and join-line in it. When we got into orbit and turned around to look at our booster and later, when we closed in during rendezvous with *Skylab*, we noticed the same thing—an unusual ability to see minute detail. In fact, objects looked so crisply and sharply defined that we got the impression we were looking at a finely-drawn animation display. It was almost unreal.

The Russian cosmonauts have noticed a significant increase in their ability to detect subtle land and ocean features and also to distinguish color differences. From their reports, they begin noticing this improved capability sometime after 100 days in space. They refer to this as "space sight" or "second sight." They have conducted controlled tests and the claim appears to be legitimate. In tests they have been able to spot features as small as thirty yards across. They have also commented that their increased visual acuity on following missions is reestablished quickly, within a couple of weeks.

117. Could you see . . . the Great Wall of China?

Yes, but we had to use binoculars. It wasn't visible to the unaided eye. The first time I thought I had seen it, I was in error; it was the Grand Canal near Beijing. Later, I was able to identify the faint line of the wall, which zigzags in a peculiar pattern across hundreds of miles.

View From Space: Egypt and Sinai Peninsula   Lake Nasser is clearly visible on the lower right side of the picture, as is the Nile running across from it to the upper left. To its right can be seem the Sinai Peninsula and the northern tip of the Red Sea. (See Question 117.)

... the Pyramids?

No. I was unable to see them even with the binoculars.

... lightning?

Yes. It is most spectacular in the equatorial regions where thunderstorms covered thousands of square miles. We could also see lightning in thunderstorms on the horizon over 1,500 miles in the distance.

Photo of San Francisco Bay Area   This photo actually shows more detail than the astronauts could see with the unaided eye. The Golden Gate Bridge (closest to the bottom left corner) and the Oakland Bay Bridge (to its upper right) are visible here. (See Question 117.)

. . . the Grand Canyon?

Yes. It was very easy to see and identify. The colors of the walls of the canyon were quite obvious. After snowfall had covered the northern and southern rims, the colors were most vivid.

. . . the Golden Gate Bridge?

No. We could see San Francisco Bay, but I was unable to see the bridge, even though I knew where it was.

. . . the Aswan Dam of Egypt?

Yes. It's quite large and stands out clearly against the desert terrain. The Nile River is also very easy to see for the same reason.

. . . the "airfields" of ancient astronauts, as popularized in books and television programs?

No. We examined the Plains of Nazca, at the foot of the Peruvian Andes near the Pacific coast of South America, but were unable to see the patterns in the plains. I took several pictures of this area and there are some very faint patterns—squares with circles inside. This is not similar to any of the patterns shown in aerial photographs of the area.

. . . lights at night?

Yes. In industrialized countries the lights are not only visible but are quite bright. Cities and major highways are very easy to see at night. The city of Kiev in the Ukraine was easy to identify because of the burning of natural-gas flares. The gas is a by-product of oil-well production.

. . . the aurora: northern and southern lights?

Yes. The aurora was the only Earth feature in which I could detect motion. The aurora patterns and colors are variable. It may be red, green, or yellow and the shape can be in the form of tubes, spikes, sheets, and sprays.

. . . meteors?

Yes. Meteors are seen as they encounter the Earth's atmosphere below your position in orbit.

118. When will ordinary people get to go into space?

The "teacher in space" program was designed to accomplish this very objective. The schoolteacher selected for this program was aboard the *Challenger* and when it exploded she died with six other astronauts. For over ten years this tragedy discouraged NASA from further attempts to send up people who were not professionally trained as astronauts. However, we all look forward to the time when we can cut the cost of launches, guarantee a high level of safety for space travel and, once again, consider letting ordinary citizens fly into space. When it comes to that point—when space tourism is possible—then kids too will be able to fly in space.

It will probably be well into the twenty-first century before this is possible. Unfortunately, the cost is so high at the present time that any "passengers" on the Shuttle must also be qualified crew members with a lot of training. On John Glenn's flight on STS-95 in October 1998 he was a test subject for a study he had proposed and he went through training for several months before the flight.

A group in St. Louis, Missouri has recently offered a $10 million prize for the first privately constructed vehicle, carrying three people, that is able to reach an altitude of 100 kilometers (62 miles), return safely to Earth and repeat the flight in two weeks. It is called "X Prize." Such a flight would not carry people into orbit but they would experience weightlessness for several minutes and have a spectacular view of the Earth.

I believe that flights into space by ordinary people will become available when private companies realize that it can become a profit-making tourism enterprise. At first it will be very expensive, probably $25,000 to $50,000 per seat. As this new industry grows the costs will drop, making a space flight achievable by all the adventurous people who crave a trip into space.

119. I've read that visitors from another world, observing the Earth from several hundred miles up, would see no evidence of man's presence. What could you see that would indicate the presence of an advanced civilization?

I believe that statement was originally made after the first pictures of Mars showed no evidence of past or present civilizations, like canals or roads or structures. I think the features we saw that gave the clearest evidence of man's presence on Earth were the lighted cities and highways at night. It is a most impressive sight, and I think they could be seen from great distances out from the Earth.

It would be interesting to observe the nightside of the Earth from the moon during an Earth eclipse of the moon. This would shield the sun and permit you to look at the full nightside of the Earth. I believe it would be possible to recognize North America or Western Europe under favorable weather conditions. Other features that might reveal the presence of man, depending on the distance of the observer, would be aircraft contrails, crop and range land patterns, the Suez Canal, reservoirs in desert areas, large airfields, and (alas!) smog pockets over large cities.

120. Is the Earth prettier from space?

On a *Skylab* space walk, we could see about 1,600 miles to the horizon and had a much wider field of view than when looking through a window from the inside of the spacecraft. We had a good view of about 200,000 square miles (within 45° of vertical) of the Earth's surface and a clear and unrestricted view of the night sky. The view of the Earth was enthralling, if not downright soul-stirring.

Once, when I had just finished passing film out to Jerry Carr, who was removing and replacing film in the solar telescopes, I looked down and noticed we were directly above Lake Michigan. I could see the city of Chicago quite clearly because of the cross-hatch pattern created by snow melt on the streets. I looked over to my left and saw the mountains of Montana on the horizon; to my right were the Appalachian Mountains—the scene was breathtaking.

The view of the Earth was so enticing that I unintentionally caused a problem with the control system of *Skylab* while I was out on that space walk Christmas Day, 1973. Jerry Carr and I had completed the film magazine retrieval-replacement for the solar telescopes and Jerry had begun a one-man task of repairing a solar telescope filter wheel mechanism. The repair job was taking a long time because the problem wasn't quite as simple as originally thought.

I was stationed at a location where the view wasn't too good, so I decided to move to the end of the telescope mount where I could see better. It had a good set of foot restraints, and when we stepped into them, the body pointed out from *Skylab* with the head in a good position to scan the Earth. The view wasn't good—it was spectacular. I was really having a ball. By leaning around, it was possible to get a view of the entire horizon. It was truly like being on top of the world, and the scene was magnificent. I leaned back and looked over my head, as Jerry had done a few minutes earlier, and got the feeling of falling he had described. It wasn't a scary feeling, but somewhat like drifting lazily upside-down and watching the world roll by.

My supreme delight, however, was shattered by comments from Ed from the inside of the *Skylab*. He was making comments about problems, half-talking to himself and half-expressing exasperation with the control system of Skylab. I could tell from his comments that the large gyroscopes were acting up. One of the three had failed while Ed and I were out on a previous space walk and we were having trouble making the two remaining gyros handle the load.

Ed was busily engaged with special computer procedures to keep the *Skylab* from going out of control. He had been so busy that he was only half-aware of my comments regarding the exquisite view from the end of the telescope mount. Suddenly, his scientific mind put it all together and he yelled at me to get back to my "hole" (workstation). Just as suddenly, I also realized the problem and I was very embarrassed because I was the cause of it. The air that circulated through my space suit flowed out through an exhaust port on a unit in front of the suit. The escaping air had the same effect as a small rocket engine and was tending to roll the entire eighty-ton Space Station. I returned quickly to my workstation to eliminate the problem and felt a bit undignified about the whole situation. One minute I was on top of the world and the next I felt as meek as a kid caught with his hand in the cookie jar.

In the meantime, Jerry was having trouble reaching far enough to work on the telescope, so I moved down to help him. I ended up holding him by his legs and shoving him headfirst into an area where he could reach the telescope and complete his work. By the time we finished our work we had been out on the space walk for seven hours. It was my last space walk and certainly had been one of the most interesting sight-seeing experiences of my life.

121. What does the Earth look like?

Astronauts in Earth orbit fly at altitudes 100–300 miles above the Earth, and although they can see the Earth's curvature on the horizon, the Earth looks similar to the view seen from high-altitude aircraft. Of course, the area in sight is much greater and features appear smaller because of the distance. Although the oceans are uniformly blue, the land surfaces differ quite a lot in color, texture, and relief; both are often covered by large tracts of clouds. Cleared range lands and cultivated agricultural regions are among the most prominent man-made features visible from Earth orbit.

In particular, the slight differences in color, soil texture, stage of growth, and use of fertilizers make the boundaries between fields quite apparent. Airfields with concrete runways, large reservoirs in arid regions, and lights at night are also easy to see. Major mountain ranges have a ribbed and ridged appearance and high peaks are snow-covered. Deserts and arid regions are prominent, distinctive, often very colorful, and usually cloud-free. They also have individual coloration and surface patterns that make them easy to distinguish. Tropical rain forests of equatorial regions are huge expanses of monotonous, mottled dark green. During the day they are frequently covered with enormous thunderstorms that extend for hundreds of miles. The view has an air of fantasy about it, and you grope for words to describe what you see. My personal reaction was one of feeling humble, awed, and privileged to be witness to such a scene.

122. What color is the Earth? What colors do you see?

The colors on land vary. Mountains in nondesert regions are usually a nondescript dark brown or charcoal; high peaks and slopes are often snow-covered. Some appear coal black, like the Black Hills of South Dakota and the interior ranges of northwestern China. Some desert mountains are reddish brown. Forests are dark, almost black, except in the equatorial rain forests of Brazil and Africa, where they appear a mottled dark green. Field crops and range lands are also dark green but lighter than the forests. New growth of field crops and grasses are a brighter green than maturing crops. The only bright-green vegetation I saw was on small tropical islands.

Coral reefs and shallows are a beautiful shade of blue-green. Many lakes are light blue or blue-green from algae growth. The Great Salt Lake in Utah is crossed by a rail-line causeway, which divides it into two separate bodies of water, one red and one green. The color difference is caused by different algae and marine organisms that have adapted to different conditions present in the separated lake.

Although the ocean, in general, is dark blue, ocean currents may appear green from marine organisms that are carried by the current. Occasionally large patches of red—red tides—appear within the green. When this happens, it creates beautiful swirl patterns of green and red in the solid-blue mass of the ocean. The Falkland Current off the coast of Argentina is an iridescent bright pea-green.

The sands of the Sahara and Arabian deserts have the most beautiful colors on the surface of the Earth. From space, these deserts look like an abstract sand painting. It is a pattern of mixed textures and varying shades of black, brown, tan, red, maroon, and orange. Much of the interior of Australia is a rusty-brown color that is uniform over wide areas. We found Australia very easy to recognize after a week in orbit and referred to it as the "red continent."

123. Where can I get space pictures?

You can contact the Center Education Program Officer or Teacher Resource Center listed in the Table, Section 3 of the Appendix, to make specific requests. A Website for viewing space imagery and pictures is: http://seds.lpl.arizona.edu Note: SEDS (Students for the Exploration and Development of Space) maintain this Website. The SEDS organization is explained under *Space-related Organizations* in the back of this book. Imagery is also available on many of the NASA Websites listed in Section 4 of the Appendix.

124. Have any astronauts seen any black holes in space?

No, not by eye. Black holes don't give off light so it would be like trying to see a black star in a black sky. Although a black hole cannot be "seen," its existence and location are based on indirect evidence such as very strong gravitational effects on nearby stars and other matter in space.

125. Can you see the moon, stars, and planets any better? Are they any brighter?

The moon, planets, and stars are a bit clearer and noticeably brighter, but you really can't see them much better than from the Earth's surface. We could see about 20 percent more stars than we could from the Earth's surface. On my first space walk, I tried to identify constellations while I was on the nightside of the Earth. At first, I was confused because I was unable to recognize familiar patterns. Although I realized I was seeing more stars than I was accustomed to seeing, it still took a few minutes before I was able to adapt to the new patterns and recognize major star groups. As you might expect, stars don't twinkle when viewed from space because the twinkle is caused by atmospheric interference when looking up at them from the Earth's surface.

126. Could you see some of the planets?

Yes. We were able to see Venus, Mars, and Jupiter.

127. What does a sunrise look like from space?

A sunrise or sunset seen from *Skylab* occurred about sixteen times as fast as one observed from Earth owing to the eastward velocity of the spacecraft. The sunrise starts as a rosy glow in the atmospheric layers on the horizon. The glow brightens and spreads outward as the red deepens and the various bands of the atmosphere brighten in white, blue, orange, and yellow. Just before the sun breaks, a bright

16 SUNRISES EACH DAY

golden-yellow blooms and shoots across the bands closest to the horizon. As the sun rises, the brilliance is dazzling and it is necessary to look away. The Earth below also changes rapidly as dawn breaks. Long shadows from hills, mountains, and clouds create eerie shading patterns for hundreds of miles. On *Skylab* there were sixteen sunrises and sunsets in each day's twenty-four-hour period.

Moonrise is also intriguing. The full moon's rise is rapid, like a sunrise. As it comes above the horizon, it appears flattened and similar to moonrise seen from Earth. However, the rising occurs so fast it looks like a bubble of air rising in water. As the moon climbs higher above the horizon, it appears to "pop" from a flattened ball into a full circle.

128. Are you always in light (or darkness)?

When in orbit around the Earth, moon, or another planet, the spacecraft is in darkness when on the nightside (the side away from the sun) and in the light on the day side (the side facing the sun). On the way to the moon or another planet, or in very high orbit above the Earth, the spacecraft would always be in light.

Of course, as you travel farther away from the sun, the amount of light received from it becomes less and less. If you traveled to Pluto, the planet farthest from the sun, the sun would only look like a very bright star.

129. How hot (or cold) is it in space?

When on a space walk in orbit or on the moon, the temperature is 250°F in the sunlight and 250° below zero in the complete shade or darkness (on the nightside of the Earth).

130. How can I find out if there is a space camp in my state?

Space-related training programs for the public are listed in the back of this book under "Space Camps." Some have programs for adults as well as activities designed for various youth-age groups.

131. How do you keep from hitting stars when you're in orbit?

The stars are far beyond our solar system, the sun, and all the planets, so there is no possibility of hitting a star. People who have observed satellites and spacecraft crossing the night sky notice that the satellites appear about the same size and brightness as many stars. This may lead them to think that stars are at similar distances. To travel to the nearest star outside our solar system would require moving at the speed of light for over four years. The speed of light is approximately 186,000 miles per second (300,000 kilometers per second).

132. How can my school get educational materials about space? Who do we write to?

In the back of this book (Section 2 of the Appendix: "Guide to Information and Resources") contains a description of the types of information and materials that are available from various NASA educational support organizations. Mailing addresses and phone numbers are listed. This section also lists several Web addresses for obtaining immediate access to various types of information. You can log on to get information such as astronaut biographies and the assembly phases of the International Space Station.

133. How do I get my school online with NASA Internet services? What kind of equipment do I need?

The "NASA K–12 Internetinitiative" is a program designed to answer your questions. If you have (or know someone who has) Internet access, full information and instructions are available at: http://quest.arc.nasa.gov Assistance is also available from the Center Education Program Officer or Educator Resource Center (for your geographic location) listed in the Table of the Appendix.

134. Is there information on the Web about Shuttle missions?

Yes. http://Shuttle.nasa.gov covers past, present, and future Shuttle missions. There is also much information about the Space Station. A listing of popular space-related Web addresses is included in the back of the book under "Guide to Information and Resources."

135. What causes the Shuttle to glow in the dark?

Shuttle glow was first noticed on the third Shuttle flight when astronauts Jack Lousma and Gordon Fullerton were taking photographs of experiment packages in the Shuttle payload bay. The Shuttle glow is a faint layer of orange glow, about eight inches thick, seen above the Shuttle's tail and aft engine pods during the nightside of the orbit. This is the outside area of the Shuttle that can be seen through

STS-88 Crew Training View Building the Space Station will require countless hours spent outside the spacecraft. Here, astronauts Jerry L. Ross and James Newman practice hooking up power and data cables using handholds located outside a simulator in the Neutral Buoyancy Laboratory (NBL).

windows from the inside; the glow actually occurs on all forward-facing surfaces.

The glow is noticeable when the Shuttle flies with its top facing the direction of flight. In this attitude the tail and pods directly impact the very thin atmosphere as the Shuttle flies through space at five miles per second. The end result of "ramming" through the space atmosphere is a dim light emitted by the gasses affected. The intensity increases significantly following the firing of attitude thrusters. The residual gases from the small rockets cause a temporary increase in the density of the atmosphere surrounding the Shuttle and increase the interactive effects causing the glow.

At about 175 miles above the Earth the space atmosphere is less than one-billionth of the density of Earth atmosphere at sea level and is composed of 20 percent molecular nitrogen (N_2) and 80 percent atomic oxygen (O). However, the rapid orbital motion is thought to cause a complex interaction of oxygen atoms and nitrogen atoms (nitrogen molecules dissociated on impact) on the cold surface of the tiles covering the tail.

The precise nature of this interaction is not fully understood, but one explanation offered attributes this to the interaction of oxygen and nitrogen, which may produce both nitric oxide (NO) and nitrogen dioxide (No_2) molecules. The energy released by these chemical reactions excites the molecules to a high energy state (excess energy). This energy may be absorbed directly by the cold tile surfaces (as heat) or—if the molecule detaches from the tile surface while still excited—it will emit the excess energy as light creating the Shuttle glow.

A fluorescent lightbulb generates light by exploiting the same principle as described above for the generation of Shuttle glow. An electric arc between the electrodes of the bulb (tube) causes the mercury vapor (gas) in the tube to emit ultraviolet light (mostly invisible). This light, in turn, excites the molecules of the phosphor coating on the inside of the tube. These molecules then release visible light (the light you see) as they return to their "unexcited" or normal state. Similarly, many forms of bioluminescence (fireflies, glowworms, fox fire, luminescent marine life, and certain bacteria) result from the same process—the emission of light from excited molecules.

For more information on Shuttle glow, refer to "Shuttle Glow" by Donald E. Hunton in *Scientific American*, November 1989. This article also includes a discussion of oxygen erosion discussed in Question 137.

136. Did *Skylab* glow? Will the (future) Space Station glow?

We did not notice glow on the outside of *Skylab*. Only a few external parts of the *Skylab* could be seen from the inside; during space walks we had a good view of the outside but I never noticed the glow even on the nightside of the orbit.

The quantity of oxygen and nitrogen in the thin space atmosphere decreases progressively as the orbital altitude increases. At *Skylab* altitude (270 miles) there may have been insufficient oxygen and nitrogen present to create a visible glow. Of course, it is possible that the glow was present and it was too dim or we were never in the right place to see it. The International Space Station will fly at about the same altitude as *Skylab*.

137. What causes oxygen erosion on the Shuttle? I thought space was a vacuum—where does the oxygen come from?

Oxygen erosion is the oxidation (and destruction) of materials caused when a spacecraft hits individual atoms of oxygen at the orbital speed of five miles per second. You could think of it as oxidation that occurs much faster than we normally observe on the Earth's surface.

At approximately 175 miles above the Earth (typical Shuttle altitude), the atmosphere is very thin compared to the atmosphere on the Earth's surface (about one particle in space for 30 billion on the Earth at sea level). Even so, there are approximately 12 billion oxygen atoms in each cubic inch of the space atmosphere at this altitude.

By comparison, the air that you are breathing as you read this contains about 400 billion particles per cubic inch. One-fifth of this is "molecular" oxygen, two oxygen atoms bound together (O_2). It is very active chemically and you are familiar with oxidation processes such as the burning of fuels or the rusting of metals. However, the oxygen in space occurs as single atoms (atomic oxygen) and it is even more active than the molecular oxygen.

As the Shuttle flies through space at five miles per second the atomic oxygen blasts the forward-facing surfaces and rapidly erodes (eats away) certain materials. Plastics and some organic compounds are eaten away more rapidly than metals. Insulation blankets, anti-reflective coatings on lenses, protective films on solar panels, and lightweight composite materials used for primary structure are especially vulnerable.

For short flights, equipment can be designed to allow for this erosion. However, for space equipment that is intended for long use in Earth orbit, careful selection and development of materials and protective shielding will be required to prevent unacceptable deterioration of components. The International Space Station is designed to last for fifteen years—the designers are including means of protecting outside equipment from atomic oxygen.

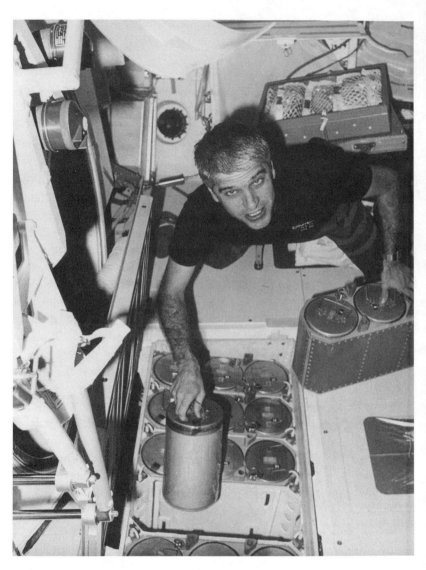

STS-40 Onboard Scene   Astronaut Sidney M. Gutierrez, STS-40 pilot, changes out the lithium hydroxide canisters on *Columbia*'s middeck. Gutierrez, making his first flight into space, was joined by six crew members for the nine-day Spacelab Life Sciences (SLS-1) mission, devoted to life sciences research. This middeck scene was photographed with a thirty-five-millimeter camera.

138. What happened to the Space Shuttle *Enterprise*?

The *Enterprise* was used for glide tests ("approach and landing" tests) in the late 1970s. It was carried "piggyback" on a modified Boeing 747 jumbo jet and released about 22,000 feet above the ground. This provided about two minutes of glide to Edwards Air Force Base. These tests were used to test Shuttle subsonic aerodynamic handling and performance as well as the Shuttle approach navigation aids at Edwards.

Originally, NASA had planned to modify the *Enterprise* for space flight but it was retired after the glide tests. Currently (1999), it is held in storage at the Dulles facility of the Smithsonian Institution near Washington, D.C. The Smithsonian has plans to exhibit the *Enterprise* when their enlarged facilities at Dulles are opened, scheduled for 2003. Incidentally, the jumbo jet used for the glide tests is now used to ferry the Shuttle back to the Kennedy Space Center in Florida when the Shuttle lands at Edwards.

139. What is a solar flare like?

It's seen as a sudden brightening of a small area on the surface of the sun. It is something like a violent thunderstorm on Earth, and it usually results in a sudden increase in radiation and particles that stream out from the sun. This increased emission can be a danger to space travelers in deep space—for example, astronauts on lunar missions or on the way to Mars.

140. What would the astronauts on deep space missions do if a solar flare happened?

Moon missions were fairly short, about eight to ten days, and the only protection for the astronauts was the spacecraft walls. In the case of a flare, they would have stayed in their command module and canceled their lunar landing, or they would have cut short their stay on the moon and returned to their command module. It provided more protection than the thinner walls of the lunar landing spacecraft. For long space flights, like a trip to Mars, the likelihood of being exposed to high doses of radiation is much greater, and special rooms or chambers must be provided to protect the crew following solar flares. These compartments are sometimes referred to as "storm cellars." (See Question 187.)

141. What did it look like when you looked into space?

The view of space from the sunlit side of the Earth is different from the view on the nightside. On the day side of the orbit, space appears as a solid background of black. The sun, moon, and brighter stars and planets are visible, but the general impression is that space is a black emptiness. On the nightside of the Earth, stars appear bright and sharp, but it seems that space is even blacker than on the day side—a vast void of outer darkness.

The effect of the nightside view of space is most dramatic when out on a space walk. I got my first unrestricted view of the entire night sky just as I had stopped working on a jammed radar antenna. Dr. Gibson and I had given up trying to use a small flashlight to continue our work in the dark. I raised the visor on my helmet cover and looked out to try to identify constellations. As I looked out into space, I was overwhelmed by the darkness. I felt the flesh crawl on my back and the hair rise on my neck. I was reminded of a passage in the Bible that speaks of the "horror of great darkness." Ed and I pondered the view in silence for a few moments, and then we both made comments totally inadequate to describe the profound effect the scene had made on both of us. "Boy! That's what I call dark."

142. Did you have any strange encounters?

No, but once Ed Gibson and I thought we were. We were on a space walk and had been working over an hour, attempting to repair a piece of equipment covered by an aluminum-coated plastic blanket. The repair work took about four hours, and we could only work when we were on the day side of the Earth, where Earth shine lighted the work area. I had been tearing off pieces of the blanket that covered an electronic box in order to remove and replace it. I had just gotten the box exposed when we noticed we were entering twilight, so we stopped working to wait for sunrise.

The Earth below was in total darkness, but we were still in faint

OVERWHELMED BY THE DARKNESS

twilight because of our altitude. I had begun looking into the night sky to continue a star-field study, when Ed said in a rather querying tone: "Look over there; are those UFO's? There are hundreds of them." I looked and saw a cloud of metallic purple-and-violet sparkling objects. The sky was black behind them and they glistened with unusual sharpness and clarity. We became rather excited as we described them

HUNDREDS OF U.F.O.s

to Jerry Carr on the inside of *Skylab*. He turned down the lights inside and looked out the window, trying to see what new and wonderful discovery we had made.

We all laughed as we realized what they were. The shreds of aluminum-coated plastic I had torn off had been blown away by the exhaust air from our space suits and had created a huge cloud of tiny reflectors several hundred yards out from *Skylab*. In the fading twilight of space they had popped into view and created a dazzling, twinkling cloud to decorate the night sky. They were still visible in twilight several hours later, after we had finished our space walk and reentered the *Skylab*. It was Thanksgiving Day, and while we had our turkey that

OTHER INTELLIGENT LIFE

evening, we were able to look out the window and see the twinkling tinsel of our unintentional Christmas decorations.

143. Do you believe there is other intelligent life in the universe?

No, or I should say I'm not convinced. It seems reasonable to believe there is other intelligent life, but "believing" does not make it so. Based upon our limited understanding of the universe and life forms, there exists the distinct possibility that intelligent life exists elsewhere in our own and other galaxies. To change this possibility into fact requires for me some sort of undisputed scientific evidence, not mere conjecture or statistical guesswork. At present, such evidence does not exist.

A project called *SETI* (Search for Extraterrestrial Intelligence) has and is being conducted to try to answer this question. It involves "listening" on certain radio frequencies to try to detect signals that have a pattern that might indicate they originated from another civilization within our galaxy. It would be an event of historic significance if they were to be successful. Thus far, the effort has had no success but it has only been in operation for a few decades.

144. What about the UFO's that accompanied our spaceships to the moon? (Astronauts have been quoted as observing mysterious objects following them on the way to the moon.)

I think the reports of astronaut sightings were misconstrued. We often observed clouds of ice crystals that formed from water and urine dumps. I know of no unexplained well-defined material objects that accompanied our spacecraft to the moon. One such report turned out to be the third stage of the Saturn booster rocket.

145. Does someone have to stay awake and on duty all the time you are in space? If not, who keeps you informed of events?

It depends on the nature of the space mission. On *Skylab* we all slept at the same time but the Mission Control Center in Houston could have awakened us in the event of a problem. We had speaker boxes in our sleep compartments so we could have responded immediately. This same approach has been used by cosmonauts on the Russian *Salyut* and *Mir* space stations. This is because the crews were small and teamwork needed to do some jobs required all the crew to be awake at the same time; it also prevented crew activity from disturbing sleeping crew members. Also, on long missions having all the crew members awake at the same time provides company and satisfies a social need.

Shuttle crews are larger and the sleep schedule is dictated by the type of mission. For Shuttle/*Spacelab* missions the crew is divided into two teams and they work twelve hours on and twelve hours off in alternating shifts, usually with three people on each team. For most non-*Spacelab* Shuttle missions the entire crew sleeps at the same time. When fully assembled, the International Space Station will have a crew of six working in alternating twelve hour shifts (three astronauts per shift), similar to the Shuttle/*Spacelab* schedule. (See Question 72.)

146. What causes the weird lightning that flashes up toward space? Could these flashes pose a danger to astronauts in space?

At this time scientists are unable to explain the cause of the flashes, which are short-lived, diffuse (fuzzy) red or blue streams of light that occur above thunderstorms. Preliminary studies indicate that the flashes are not lightning, airglow or aurora-like (northern-southern lights) phenomena. The red flashes (called "red sprites" by the scientists studying them) reach up to sixty miles and the blue flashes (called "blue jets") poke up to twenty miles above the Earth's surface. Red sprites are described as blood-red flashes with blue tendrils hanging down from some of the flashes. Blue jets are flashes that appear in narrow beams, fans, sprays, or cones of light in hues of blue or purple. Although they last only a few thousandths of a second they are clearly visible and one scientist was reported as saying, "The flashes look like the Fourth of July, like Roman candles with fountains."

These flashes have been reported by pilots and Shuttle astronauts over the last few years but the first recorded observations of these flashes above thunderstorms extend back to 1886. At this time too little is known about the energy content of the flashes to say if they pose a threat to astronauts or high-flying aircraft. The flashes generally originate above 40,000 feet, which is higher than the altitudes used by most commercial or passenger jet aircraft. One day while flying to Florida in a NASA T-38, I climbed to 46,000 feet to top a thunderstorm and—even though I was in clear air—the plane was hit repeatedly by lightning. These strikes were a real surprise to me, especially since I was getting zapped in the left knee every time it hit the plane. I don't think these strikes were associated with the blue or red flashes, but there is a lot of energetic activity above thunderstorms as well as inside and below them.

147. Does having men and women on Shuttle flights cause any problems?

Having mixed crews of men and women has caused no problems. The work pace is very demanding, the people are all dedicated professionals and they have little time to be diverted by gender-related considerations.

148. Have any married couples ever flown together in space?

Yes. Astronauts Mark Lee and Jan Davis were married during their training for Shuttle mission 47 (STS-47) and worked on different shifts during the eight-day *Spacelab* mission (12–20 September 1992).

149. Did the astronauts find evidence that others had been to the moon at some previous time? (There have been rumors that the astronauts found evidence of extraterrestrial life on the moon.)

If such evidence had been found, it would have been freely and widely publicized as a major triumph of space exploration.

150. Did we really go to the moon? I've heard that space exploration is all a hoax and is staged out in the desert for television transmission.

Yes, we went to the moon. Walter Cronkite wouldn't have lied to you. Incidentally, a man I knew for many years went to his grave believing that I had never been in space. He must have believed I was part of this "hoax." Some people have great difficulty accepting things that are beyond their power to comprehend.

What really puzzles me is the persistence of this notion. Currently (1999), there is a movement that is like a loosely organized cult that has embraced the lunar-hoax theory. They even exchange their thoughts and opinions over the Internet. They are reminiscent of the Flat Earth Society in Britain that insist the Earth is really flat and not a sphere.

151. What would happen if you looked at the sun?

Looking directly at the sun for even a moment can cause permanent injury to the eyes whether you're on Earth or in space. Don't ever do it. During space walks, we had a gold coating on our helmet visors to protect us from ultraviolet (uv) rays from the sun. This coating also reduced glare and acted like sunglasses, but it still was not enough protection to permit looking directly at the sun. On one of my space walks, I had great difficulty attempting to photograph a comet near the sun. I was supposed to aim the camera by eye and eventually was able to sight the camera and keep the sun out of my line-of-sight by getting into a position where the disc of the sun was blocked out and shaded by one of the large solar arrays.

Most spacecraft windows are especially coated to eliminate most of the uv, but some windows are built to permit removal of the uv screen (pane) for scientific observations. One cosmonaut got a sunburn just by working near the window during setup of the cameras and instruments.

152. Did you have a special Instrument for looking at the Earth? The moon? Planets? Stars?

We had many instruments for the scientific study of the Earth. These included cameras and instruments that sensed various types of radiation from the Earth's surface. One of these instruments included a viewing telescope used to guide a sensing device that detected radiation from a very small area on the Earth's surface. Small features studied by this instrument included volcano craters, unusual desert areas, lake and reservoir surfaces, forests, meadows, and copper-mine waste piles. We used this instrument to look at the moon, but only for evaluating the instrument itself. I used two instruments to make navigational sightings on the moon, stars, and the Earth's horizon, but they weren't for viewing as such. They were designed to see if a person could take manual readings accurately enough to determine spacecraft position and altitude in reference to the Earth.

The Hubble Space Telescope placed in Earth orbit by the Shuttle in 1990 is providing dramatic images of distant regions of the universe, other stars in our own galaxy and also our solar system. The Space

Station will be used for many types of Earth studies and astronomical observations.

153. If you were going five miles per second, how long did you have to look at a spot (feature) on the ground?

A general rule we developed was that we could see a feature fairly well when it was within a 550-mile circular region directly below our position. We could pick up an approaching point or feature when it was about 275 miles out in front and could track it or watch it until it was about 275 miles behind us. The diameter of the circle of "good viewing" is about twice the orbital altitude, so it becomes smaller for spacecraft at lower altitudes and the viewing time is less.

At five miles per second this means that we had about 110 seconds—or almost two minutes—to study an object that passed directly below our path. As the point passed directly below the spacecraft, it appeared to move at a rate very nearly the same as a landmark would appear to move if viewed from a jet aircraft flying at 40,000 feet above the ground. We took advantage of this similarity during our training and practiced using a telescope-tracking system mounted to the belly of a T-38 jet aircraft.

154. Did you have any experiments that were done just for fun? Did you have anything like toys just to play with?

Not exactly. We had several experiments that were thoroughly entertaining to do. Jerry Carr and I got to fly the astronaut maneuvering unit in the large forward compartment of *Skylab* (twenty-one feet in diameter and twenty-five feet high). It used nitrogen gas thrusters, so it did not pollute the air inside *Skylab*, and we test-flew the unit to evaluate its performance and to suggest design improvements. The manned maneuvering unit (MMU) used by Shuttle astronauts in the 1980s was a direct outgrowth of the device we flew inside *Skylab*.

The demonstrations we performed with water drops were originally suggested as science-support activities. However, they turned out to be so much fun that we did more than the ground scientists had requested, usually performing them on our day off or during off-duty hours.

Several items in our entertainment kit could be called toys. The action of rubber balls and darts is described in Questions 93 and 94. We also had a toy gyroscope used for science demonstrations. Jerry Carr used a string to tug it around as it floated above our wardroom table, to demonstrate the unusual properties of a gyroscope. Shuttle astronauts have taken a wide variety of toys including ball and jacks, toy magnets, tops, yo-yos, and Slinkies.

155. Would it be possible to have a baby in space?

Nobody knows for sure because it hasn't been done. However, nothing in the discoveries to date has indicated that it would not be possible. Some puzzling results were obtained on a 1989 Shuttle flight that carried thirty-two fertile chicken eggs. Sixteen had been laid two days before launch and sixteen had been laid nine days before. After the flight, the eggs were recovered and the incubation period was continued to completion on Earth. All of the nine-day eggs hatched out but none of the two-day eggs hatched.

There has been much speculation about the cause of this difference. Some have thought that the launch vibration may have been more injurious to the eggs at a younger stage of development. Others have suggested that the microgravity or weightlessness may have been the cause, preventing the yolk from settling against the shell (required for development of the embryo). Many more experiments will have to be performed to determine how weightlessness changes the way the body actually functions and especially how weightlessness would affect human embryo development.

156. Have any animals been born in space?

The second *Skylab* crew carried a plastic bag containing pregnant guppies in about a quart of water. The baby guppies were born in space and seemed to do better than their mothers in swimming. The mothers swam around in loops and strange patterns. The baby guppies seemed to swim normally.

On my flight we carried gypsy moth eggs, which hatched out in space during the mission. This experiment had a serious purpose. It was performed for the Department of Agriculture, which was trying to develop sterile moths to use in combating the infestation damage these moths cause to trees.

157. Could you smoke in space?

It probably would be possible to smoke, but it would be dangerous because of the fire hazard and undesirable because of the air pollution. I don't smoke, but some astronauts do. Most of them quit smoking several weeks before they went into space.

158. If you could smoke in space, what would happen to the smoke and the ashes from a cigarette?

The smoke would contaminate the air temporarily, but would be eventually removed by charcoal air filters. The ashes could possibly drift around and get in the eyes or be inhaled and cause irritation. It isn't the most pleasant habit to accommodate in space. Smoke (or warm air) rises on Earth because it weighs less than colder air—in space everything is weightless, so there is no force to cause the circulation we normally observe around a candle flame or bonfire. If there were no air circulation from fans, the smoke would hover in a cloud around the smoker—a just and appropriate situation.

There are no benefits to smoking but there are many bad effects. Smoking causes the body to absorb carbon monoxide, which reduces the oxygen-carrying capacity of the blood. It also causes reduced blood flow throughout the body that aggravates the penalty caused by the carbon monoxide. Both of these effects reduce a person's performance or ability to react. In addition, the long-term effects include a high probability of developing lung cancer or emphysema (breathing difficulties). A person desiring to become an astronaut should avoid smoking.

159. Who do I write to at NASA to get information for a school report?

Mail addresses, phone numbers, and Internet addresses at the NASA facility serving your area are included in the "Guide to Information and Resources" in the Appendix. Find your state in the left column and then contact the NASA person or office listed to the right. Many NASA

Websites have photographs and graphics that can be printed out in addition to text files and they are available immediately for your report. Start with the following:http://www.hq.nasa.gov/office/codef/education and www.challenger.org

160. How big was *Skylab?*

It was about 100 feet long and weighed eighty tons. The space inside was about the same as a three-bedroom house (12,500 cubic feet). After we docked to *Skylab* the entire assembly weighed about 100 tons. *Skylab* was launched by a modified moon rocket (Saturn V), which was as tall as a thirty-three-story building (330 feet) and weighed a little over 6,000,000 pounds.

161. How big was the rocket that launched you into orbit?

The Saturn 1B was about 225 feet tall and weighed 1,300,000 pounds.

162. How long did it take to build *Skylab?*

It took about six years to build Skylab, which was launched fully assembled. The Space Station modules are built separately and the assembly will require over five years.

163. What did *Skylab* cost?

Skylab cost $2.6 billion over a seven-year development period.

164. How much do astronauts earn? How much did you get paid?

An astronaut's salary depends on his or her experience and qualifications. Astronauts who are still active members of the military (on loan to NASA) receive their normal military pay. Civilian astronauts are assigned a civil service rating, if they don't already have one, and get the standard salary for that rating. Astronauts do not receive special pay or bonuses for making flights into space. However, the

Launch of *Skylab4/* Saturn 1B Booster   The *Skylab4/* Saturn 1B space vehicle launching from Kennedy Space Center in November of 1973. *Skylab* was the third and last of the scheduled manned *Skylab* missions. (See Questions 160 and 161.)

crew does receive a modest amount for space flights. I got a total of $194.65 for "incidental expenses" on our eighty-four-day mission.

165. How much did your space suit cost? Did you get to keep it? Where is it now?

About $400,000. Astronauts don't get to keep their space suits; they are used by other astronauts in training exercises. Even though they were custom-fitted, they could be adjusted to fit other astronauts of the same approximate size. The suit I used on *Skylab* is owned by the Smithsonian Institution. My training suit is used in a display at the International Space Hall of Fame at Alamogordo, New Mexico. The Shuttle suit costs over a million dollars and, because of the backpack or PLSS, is rather expensive to maintain. NASA has an effort underway to reduce the cost and maintenance expense of future suits.

A SPACESUIT COSTS $400,000

166. What kind of spacecraft did you use to go up to *Skylab?* What happens to the spacecraft after flight?

We went up to *Skylab* in a special Apollo-type command and service module. The command module separated from the service module just before reentry. Overall, it was about the size of a school bus (35 feet long, 12.8 feet in diameter) and weighed 30,000 pounds. The cabin volume—the space inside the command module for the astronauts—was about the same as the inside of a station wagon or a sports-utility vehicle.

The command module was shaped like a cone. The conical shape was similar to the shapes of the earlier Mercury and Gemini spacecraft. The heat shield covered the curved base of the cone. The overall shape was adopted because the designers had experience with it and were confident it could accomplish the maneuvering required during reentry when returning from the moon.

The Mercury-, Gemini-, and Apollo-era spacecraft were used for only one flight. After the missions they were inspected and analyzed to improve our knowledge of spacecraft and system design. Following postflight evaluation they were placed in the care of the Smithsonian Institution, which controls their loan for space exhibits.

167. After reentry, how much did the chutes slow down the command module? How fast were you dropping on the parachute at splashdown?

At approximately 30,000 feet a small parachute called a *drogue chute* was deployed to stabilize the spacecraft descent and it was released shortly before the main parachutes were deployed. The parachutes opened at 10,000 feet above the ocean and slowed our descent to about twenty miles per hour at splashdown (about thirty feet per second).

168. What kind of metal was your spaceship made of?

Most of the metal in the structure of spacecraft and rockets is aluminum. Where high strength is needed, steel, titanium, and other alloys or composite materials may be used.

169. How many pieces are in the rocket (spacecraft, *Skylab*)?

The large *Saturn V* moon rocket had hundreds of thousands of parts in the three major sections (stages). The Apollo command module had over 2,000,000 parts; *Skylab* had about 150,000 parts.

CRV Artist's Conception   This artist's conception depicts an International Space Station (ISS) Crew Return Vehicle (CRV) that may result from an innovative NASA research project at the Johnson Space Center (JSC) called the X-38. The CRV is a type of "lifeboat" for space station crew members to use for an emergency return to Earth. As much as 80 percent of the X-38 spacecraft's design would use already existing technology and already performed research, thus dramatically reducing its cost. With relatively minor modifications, the X-38 CRV design could also be used as a crew transport vehicle for launch on a variety of boosters. Atmospheric flight tests with a full-scale X-38 prototype are planned to take place at the Dryden Flight Research Facility (DFRF) in the spring of 1997.

170. How fast did you go?

We traveled at a speed of 17,500 MPH (about five miles per second) while on *Skylab*, at an altitude of 270 miles (415 km) above the Earth's surface. At a given altitude in circular orbit all spacecraft will travel at the same speed. The orbital velocity is determined by the laws of

ASTP Soviet Soyuz Spacecraft View An excellent view of the Soviet Soyuz spacecraft in Earth orbit, photographed from the American Apollo spacecraft during the joint U.S.-U.S.S.R. Apollo-Soyuz Project (ASTP) docking in Earth-orbit mission. The Soyuz is contrasted against a white-cloud background in this overhead view. The three major components of the Soyuz are the spherical-shaped Orbital Module, from which two solar panels protrude. The docking system of the Orbital Module was specially designed to interface with the docking system on the Apollo's Docking Module. The ASTP astronauts and cosmonauts visited each other's spacecraft while the Soyuz and Apollo were docked in Earth orbit for two days.

WE TRAVELLED AT 17,500 MPH
(5 MILES PER SECOND)

physics. We circled the Earth over 1,200 times during the eighty-four days we were in space, which adds up to 34,500,000 miles.

171. If you're going so fast how come it looks like you're not moving?

When you're riding along in a car the other people in the car don't appear to be moving but—to someone along the road outside the

STS-49 Landing   Space Shuttle *Endeavour* makes its first landing, following a successful nine-day mission in Earth orbit. Fully deployed here is the main chute in NASA's first exercise of its detailed test objective (DTO-521) on the drag chute system. Main gear touchdown occurred at 1:57:38 P.M. (PDT), May 16, 1992.

car—you all seem to be moving pretty fast. Also, people in other cars coming toward you look like they're going even faster, especially when they streak by you. The cameras used to take movies and television in the spacecraft are also moving along with the crew so it's like using a video camera in a moving car or plane. Later, when looking at the video playback you wouldn't be aware that the entire setting was in motion unless a scene included a view of outside objects moving past.

When you look at the ground from a spacecraft or airplane you don't appear to be moving very fast because the ground is so far away. While moving at the same speed, the lower you get, the faster the ground seems to move under you. Likewise, when riding in a car at 55 MPH the objects alongside the road seem to whiz by, but a tall building or hill a mile away seem to be almost standing still. You get the strongest sense of an object's speed when your head has to move fast to keep your eyes on it.

172. Why aren't you swept (blown) away when you go outside on a space walk? What happens if you're outside and can't get back in because you're hurt or sick?

The atmosphere or "air" around a spacecraft is very thin and doesn't exert a noticeable wind force (drag) on the astronauts when they go outside on a space walk. So there's really nothing to sweep you away. There really is a tiny amount of drag but it is extremely small and both the spacecraft and the astronaut feel the same effect. NASA rules are that there will always be two people on an EVA (space walk). This is a safety precaution to assure that, if one crew member has a problem, the other will be available to help.

173. What would happen if you floated away on a space walk?

On *Skylab* we were attached to the spacecraft with a hoselike line called an *umbilical.* It provided the breathing oxygen, fed cooling water to our liquid-cooled garments, contained the communication wires and included a steel cable to provide strength to keep us from floating away.

Shuttle astronauts use a suit that is self-sufficient and they do not require a hose connection to the Shuttle. Although it is very unlikely, if an astronaut on a space walk did float away, the Shuttle is capable of flying over to the astronaut and rescuing him or her. However, if the Shuttle happened to be docked to the Space Station when this occurred, it could be a real problem because the Shuttle cannot undock quickly. A new device, however, is now available to cover this situation. (See Question 174.)

174. When astronauts work outside to put the Space Station together is there any chance they'll slip free and get lost in space?

The assembly of the Space Station will require many space walks or EVAs. The outer surfaces of the various pieces of the Space Station will be fitted with handrails, hand holds, and sockets where foot restraints can be mounted. Also, along the planned translation paths (crawl paths) the spacing between handrails will be no more than two feet to enable comfortable reach when transferring between the rails.

However, because of the large number of EVAs and the difficulty of the jobs the astronauts will be doing, it's just possible they may drift away if they become untethered accidentally or slip free of their foot restraints. To cover this problem, NASA has developed a small jetpack that fits to the bottom of the suit backpack. It is called the *SAFER* (simplified aid For EVA rescue). It can stop tumbles automatically if the astronaut drifts away in a spin and provides small engines to enable the astronaut to fly back to the Space Station. It works like the manned maneuvering unit (MMU) but is lighter, much smaller, easier to maintain and costs less. (See Question 36.)

175. What is a graveyard orbit?

It is a long-lasting (thousands of years) orbit in a position and altitude that poses little risk of colliding with other satellites. The term usually applies to an orbit a few hundred miles above the orbit used by communication and weather satellites (22,300 miles above the Earth's surface). When satellites in this orbit approach the end of their useful life, residual propellant is used to raise them up and out of the way of other satellites so it has little chance of hitting them.

176. I thought there was a lot of room up in space. What do NASA people mean when they say that space is getting crowded?

The "crowding" usually refers to the orbital band 22,320 miles above the equator. This is the altitude at which a satellite's orbital velocity equals the Earth's rotation rate and appears stationary as viewed from the Earth. It is a prized location for communications and weather satellites. They are always in line-of-sight with their matching ground stations (a TV satellite dish, for example) so continuous transmission or reception links are possible. However, crowding occurs if satellites are less than 3° apart (angle measured from the center of the Earth). This corresponds to a separation distance of less than 1,500 miles between the satellites. If the angle is less than 3° radio signals can interfere with each other when beamed from up or down to Earth. This orbit at 22,320 miles is referred to as *geosynchronous Earth orbit* (GEO), and the term "GEO crowding" is often used to describe this problem. Currently, much effort is underway to reduce the problem and some have suggested expanding the range of frequencies allowed to these satellites. Note: The GEO orbital path is also known as the *Clarke belt*. This orbit was first proposed for use as communications-relay by British physicist, mathematician, and author Arthur C. Clarke in 1945.

177. Did you hit any meteoroids? What would happen if you did hit one?

Yes, but all were very small, the size of a tiny speck of dust. We had special test surfaces mounted outside on *Skylab* that were called *micro-meteoroid samplers*. Tiny meteoroid particles made miniature craters when they hit some of the samplers. A meteoroid larger than a pinhead (1/16 inch diameter or larger) would probably burn a hole in the wall of a spacecraft if it were not protected. Assuming no one was hit by the tiny fragments, the worst problem arising from the hole would be a loss of air. The larger the meteoroid, the worse the problem. The hazard from meteoroids is actually much less than being hit by manmade orbital debris. (See Question 194.)

Hits from micro-meteoroids have been detected on our helmets, but the tiny pits are not visible to the unaided eye. A scanning electron microscope can be used to take pictures of them. They look like miniature craters.

178. How did you generate electricity?

On *Skylab*, large surfaces called *solar arrays* were covered with small devices (solar cells), which converted sunlight into electricity. Part of the electricity generated on the sunlit side of the Earth was stored in batteries for use on the nightside. The Space Station will use large solar arrays to generate electrical power.

The command module used fuel cells that combined oxygen and hydrogen to generate electricity and water. The Space Shuttle also uses fuel cells. A fuel cell is a device that combines two chemicals to produce electricity. Spacecraft fuel cells combine oxygen and hydrogen gases to produce electricity and drinking water.

A fuel cell is like a cheese sandwich, with two porous metal plates (the slices of bread) on each side and a chemical (the cheese) in between. Oxygen is forced in through one plate and hydrogen through the opposite plate. The oxygen and hydrogen gases combine on the inside of the sandwich to form water. The water is removed as it is formed and piped to the drinking-water supply. During this chemical process, a flow of electrons occurs between the plates to create a capability to deliver electricity to the spacecraft power system. The chemical (cheese in the "sandwich") is a strong alkaline solution. Spacecraft fuel cells currently in use employ potassium hydroxide as the chemical filler for the fuel-cell sandwich.

179. How did you heat the spacecraft?

When required, electrical heaters warmed air that was circulated through *Skylab*. Most of the time, though, the need was to cool the spacecraft, because a lot of heat was produced by electrical and electronic equipment as well as by sunlight on the sides of the spacecraft. The Space Station will generate much more heat internally and has large radiators to emit the heat into space.

180. What kind of lights did you have?

On *Skylab* we had over eighty light fixtures that used fluorescent bulbs. Light fixtures in the airlock compartment and on the outside of *Skylab* were incandescent (like normal lightbulbs). For interior use, fluorescent bulbs are preferred because they give more light than an incandescent bulb using the same power. However, incandescent bulbs work better where very cold temperatures may be encountered, such as shaded areas of the exterior (during day) and the entire outside of the vehicle during the nightside portion of the orbit. The Space Station interior lights are fluorescent.

181. Did you grow any plants on *Skylab?*

Dr. Gibson grew rice plants on our mission. The purpose was to determine the growth rate and direction of stem growth in weightlessness. A light was shone on the plants continually, in an attempt to make the stems grow straight toward the light, but they sort of turned and twisted as they grew. It really looked strange.

182. Did you use plants to control the amount of carbon dioxide expired by crew members?

On *Skylab*, we did not use plants to remove carbon dioxide, but this may be possible in the future. This technique may be used on long space missions to other planets, on a permanent moon base, or in a space colony.

183. How did you control the carbon dioxide level in the spaceship atmosphere? How could you tell what it was?

On *Skylab*, we used a device called a *molecular sleve* to trap and remove carbon dioxide (CO_2) exhaled by crew members. Air was forced through the sieve, a device manufactured by pressing metal powder into a cake or solid block, which acted like a filter. The spaces between the powdered metal particles were large enough to let nitrogen and oxygen pass through, but not the large molecule of CO_2. The trapped CO_2 was vented outside the *Skylab* every fifteen minutes.

Our command module used a different system. A chemical, lithium hydroxide (LiOH), was used to absorb the carbon dioxide. The Space Shuttle also uses this method. The LiOH system is simple but requires a large number of LiOH units; as each LiOH unit becomes saturated it must be replaced with a fresh unit. Thus, an increasing number of units are required for longer missions. Later improvements on the Shuttle will replace the LiOH with a regenerable system that does not require frequent replacement units.

Technology is available to break down the carbon dioxide to recover the oxygen for replenishing oxygen supplies on board spacecraft. This technique may be added to the Space Station later. It will be a necessity for lunar bases and Mars missions.

All spacecraft have an instrument that measures the concentration (amount) of carbon dioxide in the cabin atmosphere. If this concentration becomes too high it can cause illness, rapid breathing, or unconsciousness. An average-size adult will consume about two pounds of oxygen per day and exhale a bit over two pounds of carbon dioxide.

184. What is a *window* in space?

Of course, we have windows in the manned spacecraft and they are necessary for certain space tasks such as photography, docking, and many other jobs. They also provide the astronauts with a view of the Earth that is valuable for Earth studies and fun viewing (space tourism).

Many times you hear the term *window* or *window of opportunity*, used by people describing the launch or upcoming events throughout the mission. When the word *window* is used in this way it usually refers to a period of time that's best for doing something. For instance, your "lunch window" may be between 11:30 A.M. and 1:00 P.M. Before 11:30, you're not hungry; if you have to wait 'til after 1:00 you may get a headache.

A "launch window" is similar and is calculated so that the spacecraft will get into space at the right position at the right time to perform some task. The "window" may be described as *narrow* or *wide*. A *narrow launch window* means that the launch must take place within a few minutes of the planned time; a *wide launch window* means that a delay of hours may be acceptable.

Other events such as satellite release from the Shuttle or scientific observations with astronomical instruments must also be done within certain time limits. *Windows of opportunity* may be described for these jobs too.

185. How much radiation exposure did you get?

I got a total of forty rems, which is about 1,200 times what I would have received on the Earth's surface during the same eighty-four day period. This was about one-quarter the maximum allowable dose. I received most of it while outside *Skylab* on space walks. The radiation was measured by personal dosimeters—also called *film badges*—that were carried on our clothing and space suits. There were also two other instruments used from time to time for measuring radiation levels at special locations inside *Skylab*.

186. Could you tell when you were receiving the radiation?

Normally you would not be aware of receiving moderate doses of radiation any more than you would feel the effects of an X ray at the dentist, or one taken by a doctor to check for broken bones. However, the radiation does cause damage to body tissue and exposure should be kept as low as possible.

Sometimes the presence of radiation can be detected by astronauts. When we were sleeping or when our eyes were dark-adapted, we could tell when we passed through zones of high levels of radiation. You begin to see light flashes even though your eyes are closed. As you first enter such an area, the light flashes are infrequent and are "seen" as streaks, point flashes, and occasionally appear as bursts. It's like watching a miniature fireworks display. Then, as you approach the more intense region of this zone, the flashes become more frequent and varied. When passing through the "hottest" part, the effect is almost dazzling and it looks like your entire field of vision is filled with sparkling points, streaks, and bomb bursts.

The area where this occurs is called the *South Atlantic Anomaly* (SAA); it is a depression or low spot in the radiation belts that are created by the Earth's magnetic field. The magnetic field traps and holds certain ionized or charged particles, mostly electrons and protons. The Earth's magnetic poles do not coincide with the Earth's axis of rotation or geographic poles. This mismatch causes this irregularity or low spot in the belts.

Light flashes were also noted on the Apollo missions to the moon and were caused by the same particles mentioned above. Many of the earlier orbital flights (Mercury and Gemini) were close to the equator and the altitude was too low to encounter the South Atlantic Anomaly, so they didn't see the flashes. Once the Apollo flights were on their way to the moon they were beyond the protective shield of the radiation belts around the Earth and were exposed to the direct emission of solar particles. Many noticed the light flashes described previously, but they were very reluctant to report them. They were probably afraid the doctors would think they had a serious neurological problem since no one had even suggested such a peculiar effect might occur.

It wasn't until after several had left NASA that the stories about the light flashes began to filter back to the rest of us. For the *Skylab* we were well-briefed on them and were very grateful. If we had noticed them without being told ahead of time we probably would have kept our mouths shut, too.

187. How do protect yourself to keep from getting too much radiation?

One of the most difficult problems to solve when planning for long-duration missions is providing radiation protection for the crews. In Earth orbit below the radiation belts (less than a 300-mile altitude), the problem isn't too serious because the Earth's magnetic field acts as a shield. However, on a moon base or during a mission to Mars there is a high probability of receiving large and excessive radiation doses.

Under such conditions protective measures (shielding) will have to be included. On a moon base, lunar soil can be piled over the base structures to act as a shield. On Mars missions, on the outbound and return legs, the spacecraft structure and other provisions within the spacecraft must be designed to shield the crew. We still don't understand a lot about the radiation risk, how to predict when large emissions from the sun will occur, and the best way to protect the crew. (See Question 140.)

188. Does the radiation affect spacecraft equipment?

Yes. Radiation in the form of ultraviolet or X-ray radiation can cause coatings (paint) to discolor and the more powerful (energetic) X rays can affect the performance of electronic equipment. Radiation in the form of energetic particles such as electrons, protons, and atomic nuclei can also damage electronic components or alter the memory of computer devices. The extent of the damaging effects on electronic components has become more significant as they have become smaller.

To prevent damage to such devices, the designs may be protected or "hardened." Protected designs may include some kind of shield (to intercept or neutralize the radiation) or the use of materials or circuits that are less vulnerable to radiation damage. Optical circuits that use light instead of electricity are being developed to reduce the damage risk arising from radiation effects.

189. Where does space begin?

Earth is really a part of space, but we tend to think in terms of "outer space" as beginning at some distance away from the Earth. Countries using the metric system of measures define space as starting at 100 kilometers (sixty-two miles) above the Earth. We in the United States say that a person has been "in space" if he or she goes more than fifty miles above the Earth (approximately 265,000 feet). However, during reentry, the spacecraft actually starts to "feel" the Earth's atmosphere at about seventy-five miles above the surface of the Earth (about 400,000 feet). We call this altitude the "entry interface." There are all sorts of practical terms of reference for everyday flight-planning purposes.

We might say that we enter outer space when nature's rules of orbits have much greater influence on the vehicle than do nature's rules of travel in the atmosphere. Scientists sometimes define "deep space" as an atmosphere containing one hydrogen atom per cubic centimeter (about 15 per cubic inch). At 150–175 miles above the Earth the atmosphere contains about 1,000,000,000 particles (atoms or molecules) per cubic centimeter, mostly oxygen and nitrogen atoms. Thus, the Shuttle and other spacecraft at this altitude are actually moving very fast through a very thin atmosphere.

At 175-miles altitude the Shuttle, for example, would create a drag of about one-millionth of the force of gravity (or about a quarter of a pound of drag force in the case of the Shuttle). The slight resistance to movement through this thin air not only causes space objects to gradually fall out of orbit but can rapidly damage materials on the

WHERE DOES SPACE BEGIN?

spacecraft and create a peculiar glow surrounding parts of the structure. (See Questions 135 and 136.) The effects of the Earth's atmosphere extend beyond the orbit of the moon before the near-perfect vacuum of interplanetary space is reached.

190. What does it look like when you're going up?

As the rocket climbs vertically, the sky gradually turns from blue, to dark blue, then to dark violet, and finally to jet-black at about 100,000 feet above the Earth. As the rocket gradually noses over to a level path, it is possible to see the Earth's horizon and the Earth. It is very surprising the first time you see the horizon because the layer of air—our Earth's atmosphere—looks so thin. I used to think of it as a thick blanket, but now I think of it as a thin sheet. If one could imagine an apple as big as the Earth, 99 percent of the atmosphere would be contained in a layer thinner than the skin of the apple.

191. What keeps you in orbit?

A British scientist, Sir Isaac Newton, gave a very good explanation of an orbit back in the seventeenth century. Suppose you are standing at the North Pole of the Earth and looking south toward Canada and the United States. Further, suppose you can throw a ball as fast as you desire and that air drag doesn't exist. First, you throw the ball and see it land in Hudson Bay, Canada. Not satisfied, you wind up and throw it faster and see it land in Lake Michigan. The third ball is even faster, and you see it land in the Gulf of Mexico. The fourth ball is faster yet and falls in Argentina. Finally, you really put your back into it and the ball doesn't even touch the surface of the Earth as it goes over the Antarctic and the South Pole. As you stand there considering what happened to the ball, it suddenly whizzes past your shoulder from behind you and streaks toward the south again.

What happened is, you threw it hard enough to send it all the way around the Earth. In other words, you put it into orbit. It is actually falling, but it is going so fast that its path of fall is the same as the curvature of the Earth. If there were no air resistance and the Earth were a uniform spherical mass, the ball would continue to "fall," or orbit, indefinitely. This is why a spacecraft can stay in orbit for a long time without running the engines. It is actually "falling" and is still being pulled by Earth's gravity, but its great speed keeps it from taking a path that would cause it to hit the Earth's surface.

The orbital lifetime of a satellite depends on several factors: (1) its distance or altitude above the Earth (moon, planet, sun, etc.), (2) the shape of the orbit, (3) the density of the atmosphere, and, perhaps, (4) the shape, and density of the satellite. For example, the Earth is in orbit around the sun and it will remain in orbit around the sun for billions of years. A satellite in orbit above the Earth at an altitude of about 100 miles will only stay in orbit for a few weeks or months. *Skylab* was in orbit at an altitude of 270 miles and it stayed up for six years.

192. Don't the rocket engines pollute the atmosphere and space?

Many rockets use hydrocarbon compounds or petroleum-derived fuels in the first stage, and some pollutants are produced. The upper stages usually employ liquid hydrogen and liquid oxygen that are very clean, so very little pollution is caused in the Earth's upper atmosphere or in space. The attitude rockets and orbital maneuvering engines on the orbiting vehicle cause a small amount of pollution in the form of oxides of nitrogen.

193. How much pollution is caused by a launch?

For the Space Shuttle, many tons of aluminum oxide (AlO_2) and hydrochloric acid (HCl) are produced by the solid rockets. The liquid propellant engines in the orbiter produce virtually no pollution. All rocket engines utilize combustible propellants and there are exhaust products. Some of the products are considered pollutants; others are not. For example, the exhaust products from hydrogen-oxygen used by the Shuttle's main engines are water, plus some free oxygen and hydrogen; the exhaust products from RP1 (kerosene) and LOX (liquid oxygen) used in the first stage of a Saturn rocket include carbon monoxide, carbon dioxide, water, carbon, and some unburned kerosene (hydrocarbons).

The engines used in orbit to control attitude and make adjustments to the orbit and for deorbit use nitrogen tetroxide (N_2O_4) and monomethyl hydrazine (CH_3NHNH_2). The products of combustion of these propellants include oxides of nitrogen, carbon monoxide, carbon dioxide, ammonia, water, and free hydrogen, oxygen, and nitrogen.

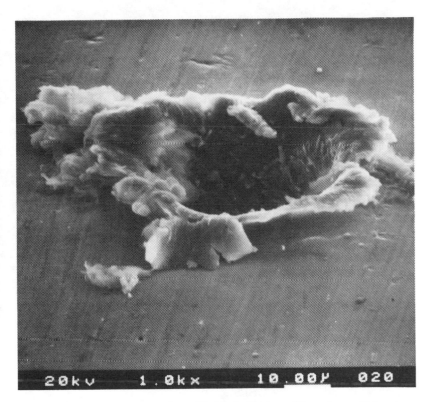

Space Debris Impact Crater Seen Through Electron Microscope This microscopic impact crater was found on a satellite returned to Earth in 1984. It is an example of the effect that tiny particles of space debris, traveling at enormous speed, can have when they hit a spacecraft's exposed surfaces. (See Questions 177 and 194.)

194. How much junk have we left in space? Isn't this dangerous? What would happen if you hit a piece of junk (manmade debris from earlier space missions)? How do you protect against this (a debris strike)?

Currently (1999) the U.S. Space Command monitors over 8,000 objects larger than four inches (10 cm) that drift in space. The altitude of these objects may be as low as 150 miles or as high as 1,200 miles. There are thousands of pieces smaller than this. The combined mass of all this debris is almost 5,000,000 pounds (2,000,000 kilograms).

The large pieces vary from payload shrouds (launch covers) to derelict spacecraft. The tiny pieces vary from paint flecks chipped off rockets, to particles of aluminum oxide (used in solid-rocket motors). By contrast, the total mass of natural "junk" or meteoroids in this same region is only 500 pounds (200 kilograms).

This space debris is definitely a hazard. Colliding with a large piece could destroy the spacecraft. These pieces may approach the spacecraft at speeds ranging from slow drift (virtually zero velocity) up to 10 miles per second (16 km per second).

The smaller pieces (larger than $1/10$ inch) may penetrate the spacecraft wall and cause a leak. Depending on the size, makeup (density), and relative velocity of the object, the leak may require patching of the spacecraft wall and repair of equipment damaged outside and inside. Or—if the hole is large enough—the collision may force the crew to abandon the damaged module.

For short-duration missions the probability of a major debris collision is quite low. However, on several occasions the Shuttle's windows have been damaged by hitting small particles such as paint flecks. The International Space Station is being designed for a space lifetime of fifteen years. Thus, the designers are rightly concerned for the safety of the crew and several protective or preventive measures are being included in the design.

1. The crew modules are attached to the Space Station framework so that the long dimension of the cylinders (cans) are pointed in the direction of motion (flight vector). This reduces the area facing the direction of flight, which decreases the likelihood of collision.
2. Crew modules considered to be the most exposed to hits will be protected with two M-D (micro meteoroid-debris) shields. The outer or primary debris shield is an outer shell or metal skin about $1/25$ inch thick that stands about six inches outside the structural wall of the crew module. About two inches below the outer shield is the intermediate or secondary debris shield, a thick blanket similar to a flak jacket. When an object strikes the outer shield it explodes from the heat generated by impact, producing a large number of smaller particles that spread out into a cone-shaped spray. This spray of smaller particles then hits the

intermediate debris shield blanket and, because they are spread out over a larger area, the blanket stops them before they strike the pressure wall of the Space Station module. This system is designed to protect the crew against hits by an object up to a two-inch diameter.

3. Ground radar and a computer tracking system will provide alerts to the Space Station when the system considers a piece of debris to be a threat. Such a system could provide a warning days or weeks in advance of the impending strike.

4. A collision avoidance system will be included to enable the Space Station to maneuver out of the way of approaching debris.

195. Did you have 100 percent oxygen in *Skylab*?

No. *Skylab* had a mixture of 75 percent oxygen and 25 percent nitrogen at a total pressure of five pounds per square inch (about 1/3 sea-level pressure).

The atmosphere of the Shuttle and the Space Station must be the same to simplify operations after docking. The pressure must be the same when they open the hatches between them. Their atmospheres are roughly equivalent to sea level (14.7 pounds per square inch) and composed of 80 percent nitrogen and 20 percent oxygen.

196. If the Shuttle is airtight, how does the "no-gravity" leak in?

The weightless (no-gravity) condition doesn't happen because of anything in space so it doesn't "leak in." In fact, you can get the no-gravity effect on Earth. Suppose you were in an elevator on the 100th floor of a tall building and the elevator fell freely for fifty floors (500 feet) before the emergency system stopped the fall to prevent injury. While you were falling the first fifty floors (about 5 1/2 seconds), you would be weightless (wouldn't feel the effect of gravity). With a gentle push you could float from ceiling to floor or wall to wall. You could also move a heavy suitcase very easily using a couple of fingers. However, once the elevator began to slow down, your body weight would start to increase, you could stand on the floor once again and, after the elevator stopped, your weight would be the same as before you started the scary ride.

In space, it's like being in the falling elevator, except the "fall" continues for the entire time you're in space. This condition is sometimes referred to as *free-fall* and is just another way of saying you're in weightlessness. Note: The weightless or free-fall condition experienced in space flight may also be referred to as *zero-g, zero-gravity, low gravity,* or *microgravity*. The term *microgravity* is used by scientists and technicians.

197. Where is the NASA room where they can cancel gravity and make people float?

There is no such room. This is a common question that arises because people have seen the movies and videos taken during training exercises in an aircraft as it performs a zero-gravity maneuver. The weightless (zero-gravity) condition only lasts for about twenty-five seconds. This maneuver is performed by a KC-135 (similar to a Boeing 707 jet airliner) especially outfitted for weightless evaluation of equipment, crew tasks, and for crew familiarization with the weightless effect they will encounter in space. Most all the seats are removed to create a large open-cabin area.

To execute this maneuver the plane dives to pick up speed, pulls up rather quickly to a nose-high climbing attitude, and then noses over gradually until reaching zero-gravity (things just start to float off the floor). The plane continues to nose over until it reaches a steep diving attitude and then pulls up gradually to start a new maneuver. While the plane is doing the nose-over (lasting 20–25 seconds), the cabin, the people, and all the equipment behave as if in space weightlessness.

Of course, many photographs, video, and movies are taken to record the training sessions and equipment tests. Because the cabin looks like an open room, these photos and videos viewed by the public have led some to believe that the scenes occurred in a room on the ground.

198. Is this the plane the astronauts call the *vomit comet*?

Yes, the astronauts and technicians that fly in it call it that. During a single training session the KC-135, also referred to as the *K-Bird*, may

The "Vomit Comet" This Boeing KC-135 is used to create short periods of weightlessness. The roller-coaster-like path created by the successive climbs and dives of the aircraft eventually causes nausea in the passengers, hence its unflattering nickname. (See Questions 197 and 198.)

execute over fifty of these pull-up and pushover maneuvers described above. After several of these maneuvers some people develop nausea. When I first began participating in these flights I could tolerate over fifty of these maneuvers without getting ill. After training in flights over many years my tolerance decreased so that, near the end of my astronaut career, I could only do about thirty-five before I began to feel queasy.

199. What was it like during reentry?

Our reentry began in darkness. Before we even felt the slowing effect of the atmosphere, the spacecraft became surrounded by a faint white "cloud." As the air friction increased, the white cloud changed to pink, then deepened to rose, and finally became a fiery mix of orange and red with streaks of bright-red particles from the heat shield in the trail of hot gases behind the spacecraft. As the thrusters fired to roll the spacecraft for corrective maneuvers, the rocket plumes caused wild swirls in the hot gases, and the patterns of flame seemed to spiral crazily along the edges of the wake of fire. The whole thing lasted about four minutes, during which we were subjected to a peak force about four times our own weight. It was such a fascinating and beautiful display that I didn't even notice the buildup of heavy force on my body. Then it seemed like it was suddenly over, and we were falling down through 100,000 feet in a gradually steepening trajectory. The rest was just procedures—the real fun was over.

200. Do the Shuttle astronauts also see this fireball during reentry?

Not exactly. Shuttle pilots beginning reentry in the dark notice an indistinct white glow surrounding the nose and cockpit areas of the Shuttle as they start reentry and it changes to a pinkish color as the heat builds up. When they enter daylight the glow is no longer visible. Another effect that occurs during the Shuttle reentry is a tubular, snaky trail of glowing gas that forms above the Shuttle, aft of the cabin, and extending back and up above and toward the tail. This "glow pulsing" during reentry was first photographed during the eighth Shuttle mission and is a most unusual effect.

201. How do you stay cool and comfortable during reentry heating?

The heat shield is a very effective insulation material, so very little heat passes through to the inside. Even though the temperature may reach 8,000°F on the heat shield, the inside of the spacecraft remains comfortable. The Shuttle uses a different system to protect the spacecraft during reentry heating. (See Question 212.)

202. What did it feel like when you entered gravity again?

Everything felt very heavy, including our own bodies. I picked up a three-pound camera just after splashdown and it felt like it weighed fifteen or twenty pounds. When I rolled over on my side in the spacecraft couch to pick up the camera, it felt like one side of my rib cage was collapsing onto the other. These exaggerated impressions of heft and weight only lasted a few days and, for the most part, disappeared completely in less than a week.

203. Did you have any difficulty adjusting to gravity again?

1. We were able to walk, but were a bit unsteady at first. I involuntarily turned to the right even though I was looking straight ahead and trying to walk straight. I also drove off the right shoulder of the road twice during my first week back. It was as if I were watching someone else drive—a weird and confusing sensation. One passenger suggested that NASA was putting something in our Tang. I was a bit upset because I didn't understand what was happening, and after I drove off the road the second time, I was very careful. This "right turn" tendency went away after the first week. I didn't tell the doctors for fear that they might ground me or use me as a guinea pig for more medical tests. I haven't had any further problems with this since the first week following the flight.
2. Almost all of the astronauts have dropped things during the first few days after return. In weightlessness, they had become used to releasing objects and having them float nearby until needed again. This was a great convenience in performing even simple tasks. I dropped the toothpaste tube and I almost dropped a glass of water on the bathroom floor the first morning after return. I felt it slipping in my fingers and gripped it again just in time. This tendency also goes away in a few days.
3. Another problem I noticed was a tendency to fall or roll out of bed. The NASA doctors got smart fast on this one. The beds we used on the aircraft carrier that picked us up were fitted with side rails. I thought this was ridiculous when I saw it. I was wrong. I

tried to "float" out of bed that night, and the rail saved me from a fall.

4. Heaviness in bed was another post-mission sensation. It felt like I was collapsing the bed when I lay down—as if I weighed several hundred pounds. The pressure distributed on my body from my weight seemed excessive for about four or five nights.

5. On the third night after my return, I struggled out of bed to go to the bathroom and I got lost in the dark. I was turning to the right again.

204. How long does it take to get back to normal?

After our eighty-four-day flight, it took about five weeks for our bodies to return to our normal pre-mission physical condition. A Russian physiologist reported that cosmonauts Vladimir Titov and Moussa Manarov readapted to the Earth environment within two months of completing a record 366 days in orbit (December 21, 1987 to December 21, 1988).

205. How many engines are on the Shuttle?

Fifty-one engines are used by the Space Shuttle vehicle:

1. Two solid rocket booster (SRB) engines, with 2,600,000 pounds thrust each, used during the first two minutes of launch.

2. Three orbiter main engines, with 470,000 pounds thrust each (vacuum), for launch only.

3. Two orbital maneuvering system (OMS) engines, with 6,000 pounds thrust each, for orbit insertion, orbital maneuvers, and deorbit.

4. Thirty-eight primary reaction control system (RCS) engines, with 900 pounds thrust each, to control the Shuttle attitude in orbit and make small translations.

5. Six vernier (fine control) RCS engines, with twenty-five pounds thrust each, to make small adjustments in attitude.

206. How long does it take to get a Shuttle ready for launch? Why does it take so long to get a Shuttle ready for launch? When will it be possible to fly the Shuttle like an airline flies passenger airplanes?

A normal prelaunch flow at the Kennedy Space Center takes about sixty-five days. To get the Shuttle ready for the next flight over 10,000 separate preparation tasks must be done. These tasks require about 40,000 man-hours by technicians. The Shuttle will never be able to fly like an airline passenger aircraft. It's just too complicated and many safety requirements must be satisfied to assure a safe launch.

207. What is the most people the Shuttle can carry?

It can carry a maximum of ten for rescue missions. Seating can be provided for a crew of three (rescue crew) and seven passengers (the crew being rescued).

208. How much does the Shuttle weigh at liftoff?

The Space Shuttle vehicle weighs approximately 4,400,000 pounds at liftoff. The Space Shuttle orbiter, the reusable spacecraft, weighs from 200,000–240,000 pounds, depending on payload carried.

209. How much can the Shuttle carry into space?

As originally designed, the Shuttle could carry as much as 65,000 pounds to equatorial circular orbits up to 230 miles. Smaller payloads could be delivered to circular orbits up to 690 miles. The higher the orbit, the less payload that could be carried—because the extra weight of fuel (propellant) needed to go higher must be subtracted from the payload weight. Also, for launches aimed to carry the Shuttle nearer to the Earth's polar regions, the payload capability must be reduced (to 32,000 pounds) because the Earth's rotation doesn't contribute to the launch. (See Question 241.) Following the *Challenger* disaster, the Shuttles were modified with many changes that added weight to the Shuttle, reducing the maximum payloads about 20 percent.

210. Why does the Shuttle do a roll maneuver just after launch? Why does it fly upside down as it's going up?

The Shuttle is held in a fixed or standard position on the launchpad with the back of the Shuttle facing east (approximately). Depending on the mission requirements the Shuttle may launch due east straight out over the Atlantic, or northeast roughly along the east coast of the United States. The Shuttle rolls in order to place the tail straight down as it reaches the heading or direction for the particular mission. This direction is called the *launch azimuth*. The roll maneuver is started as soon as the Shuttle clears the launch tower so it can complete the roll before air loads build up as the Shuttle accelerates. This keeps the air load on the tail from becoming too great.

The Shuttle launches "tail down" or upside down because the aerodynamic performance is better (it flies better that way), and it is in a better attitude to do an emergency-return maneuver if serious problems occur. Another advantage to the inverted attitude is that the Shuttle's forward windows (windshield) face downward, giving the commander and pilot a view of the horizon. On launches up the U.S. east coast the pilot has a great view of the land from North Carolina to Massachusetts.

Older spacecraft launched upside down as well. For them it was essential to have a view of the horizon in case of certain launch emergencies such as booster-rocket failures. This allowed them to maneuver the spacecraft to required attitudes by aligning marks (lines) on the hatch window with the Earth's horizon. Using these window marks the crew could position the spacecraft to thrust on into orbit with the spacecraft engines after separating from the launch rocket, or to deorbit for an emergency landing. Other window marks were used as a reference to roll the spacecraft during reentry to steer for a landing site and to reduce reentry heating.

211. When you blast off from Earth, do you use earplugs because of the noise?

No. The earphones in the astronauts helmets help reduce the launch noise but it's still quite loud.

212. Why doesn't the Shuttle use a heat shield like the older spacecraft?

The old heat shields actually burned away during reentry; thus, they could only be used once. Because the Shuttle is designed to make many flights into space and back again to Earth, it would be very expensive to put on a new shield for each flight. They designed a new surface made up of tiles called the *thermal protection system* (TPS) or *reusable surface insulation* (RSI).

On a few of the early Shuttle flights some of the tiles were shaken loose from the upper surface during the launch and boost phase. In these problem areas the tiles have been replaced by *advanced flexible reusable surface insulation* (AFRSI), a heat-resistant fabric. Occasionally the Shuttles continue to experience minor tile damage during boost. Most of this is in the form of gouges and scratches thought to be caused from ice chunks broken off the cold external tank by the shock effect created when the solid rocket motors are jettisoned (about two minutes after liftoff).

213. What are the tiles made of?

They're made of a silicon compound coated with a ceramic material that protects the tiles so they aren't damaged by reentry heating. They are designed to last the life of the Shuttle spacecraft or for 100 reentries through the Earth's atmosphere. The AFRSI fabric is a quilted blanket of heat resistant felt coated with a white silicon material.

214. How do the tiles work to dissipate or reject heat?

The tiles get rid of 95 percent of the reentry heat by radiation (rapidly emitting the heat generated by entry heating). The remainder of the heat is slowly conducted into the tile, and some of this heat diffuses out to be re-radiated after landing. A very small amount— about one percent—actually reaches the metal skin of the Shuttle.

215. What would happen if a lot of them came off?

It could cause the loss of the Shuttle during reentry. As noted in Question 212, on several of the early Shuttle flights some tiles were lost on the upper surface near the tail. These were not in a critical area and the missing tiles caused no serious problems during reentry. When a large piece of tile is broken off from the bottom side of the Shuttle the problem is more serious and may cause severe heating of the structure underneath.

216. How hot do the tiles get during reentry?

Although designed to tolerate a peak temperature of 2800°F, the highest temperature thus far experienced has been 2280°F.

217. How long a runway does the Shuttle need?

The Shuttle can land on a 10,000-foot runway, but it is better if the runway is 15,000 feet long. Many large civilian and military airfields have 10,000-foot runways. Because the Shuttle does not have engines it can use during landing, the longer runway makes it easier for the pilot to plan his landing.

218. Can it land on any airfield the right size?

Yes, but only a few airfields have all the special radio equipment to help guide the Shuttle toward the airfield. Although it would be possible to land on airfields with runways of sufficient length, such a landing would not be attempted except in an emergency.

219. How did you feel about the *Challenger* explosion? How could that happen? What can we do to make sure it doesn't happen again?

Quite frankly, I couldn't believe what I was seeing. I was numb. I had met several of the crew members during visits to the Johnson Space Center; I didn't feel like talking about the accident for several days. All astronauts know that such disasters are possible but much of the anguish was aggravated by the revelations that it was a preventable accident.

We cannot guarantee that accidents will not happen in space any more than we can manufacture and operate aircraft or cars with a guarantee that accidents with them will not occur. The expensive lesson of *Challenger* is that we must do everything reasonable to reduce the probability of such a disaster. This includes keeping safety considerations as a number-one priority during preparation for space missions. (See Question 98.)

220. Can the Shuttle astronauts use parachutes? Do they have ejection seats? How do they bail out?

Yes. The Shuttle astronauts do have parachutes. Following the *Challenger* disaster in January 1986, a bail-out system was developed to enable the astronauts to parachute from the Shuttle below 30,000-feet altitude. For launch and entry the astronauts wear partial pressure suits, called *launch and entry suits* (LES). They are not space suits—rather, they are similar to those used by the crews of high-altitude aircraft. This suit assembly includes a parachute, life raft, an emergency oxygen supply, and a clip for attaching to an escape pole that can be extended about nine feet out through the side hatch of the Shuttle.

If a bail out is required the procedure is as follows: Astronauts are already wearing their LES for entry. As the Shuttle descends through 40,000 feet the cabin is depressurized (air is allowed to leak out) to equalize the inside and outside pressure. At 31,000 feet the side-hatch door is ejected and the telescoping escape pole is extended out the hatch above the left wing of the Shuttle. With the Shuttle on autopilot, the astronauts attach clips on their suits to the escape pole. When ready to bail out (approximately 25,000 feet), the astronauts jump out at fifteen-second intervals and the clip (ring) slides along the pole to guarantee that their path clears the wing of the Shuttle. About three seconds after bail out a small (4-½-foot diameter) drogue chute is deployed automatically to stabilize the crew member during fall to 14,000 feet. At this altitude the main parachute opens automatically for the descent to the surface. Although this new system is primarily designed as protection against launch emergencies, it could also be used during descent following entry.

There are no ejection seats on the Shuttle. Note: The Shuttle *Columbia* had two ejection seats for the first four Shuttle flights. These were considered experimental test flights and were flown by a crew of two, the commander and pilot. The ejection seats were provided for emergency escape because the Shuttle had not been proven. The ejection seats were removed during retrofit (overhaul) in 1984, after the test flights and before flights were begun with four or more crew members. There isn't enough room in the Shuttle to fit in ejection seats for the larger number of astronauts, which may vary from four to eight.

221. What is the name of the Shuttle that was built to replace the *Challenger*?

The name of the replacement Shuttle is *Endeavour*, named after the ship commanded by the British astronomer and explorer Captain James Cook. Yes, this is the correct English spelling for the name (as used for Captain Cook's ship).

222. Will it be possible to rescue Shuttle astronauts if they can't get back from space? If there were an emergency, how soon could you send help?

Rescue might be possible if circumstances were just right, i.e., if a Shuttle were in the late stages of preparation for launch when another Shuttle became stranded in space. Even then a rescue launch might take as long as a week. The crew in space can extend survival time while awaiting rescue by conserving oxygen and other consumables. Estimates by NASA technicians are that the stranded crew can survive a week for each day's worth of oxygen budgeted for average flight activity. Oxygen is used to generate electricity in the fuel cells in addition to replenishing the living compartment atmosphere.

Currently, private groups are studying the possibility of establishing international procedures for rescue. This would include the U.S.,

Russia, ESA (European Space Agency), Japan, and China. Russia has the most highly developed launch capability to execute a rescue mission on short notice. NASA is developing a crew return vehicle for use on the Space Station and it is scheduled to be available by 2004. (See Question 225.)

223. Is it true that the Russian flight planners depend on the U.S. as an emergency landing area? What happens to you if you have to land in a foreign country? Is it true that you have to carry a passport in case you land in foreign country?

Yes, one of the best contingency (emergency) landing areas for cosmonauts is in the midwestern area of the United States. Since the 1970s the Russians have included this area in their candidate sites for emergency landing of spacecraft. Some orbits do not permit landing in Russia if an immediate reentry is required. The Midwest is relatively flat, which is safer for the Russian spacecraft that come down by parachute. Years ago, most nations agreed that space crews making emergency landings in or near their geographic borders would be given assistance and safe passage to return to their home countries. For each Shuttle launch, emergency landing sites are picked in case they don't make it all the way to orbit, and the Shuttle is capable of making a landing at many large airfields around the Earth. (See Questions 217 and 218.) Astronauts and cosmonauts do not have to carry passports.

224. Who was the cosmonaut that the Russians left stranded in space for five months?

Cosmonaut Sergei Krikalev launched aboard Soyuz TM-12 to the *Mir* space station on 18 May 1991 and was scheduled to return in October 1991, a mission of approximately five months. Funding difficulties in June and July of 1991 forced mission planners to rearrange the schedule and form a single mission (crew) from two that had been planned. This crew included only one cosmonaut qualified for a long stay on the *Mir* (Alexander Volkov), so cosmonaut Krikalev was asked if he would stay aboard Mir with Volkov until the next scheduled visit in March. He agreed. However, political events overshadowed this straightforward but significant rearrangement of the flight schedule.

In August 1991 an attempt was made to overthrow the government of the U.S.S.R. by Soviet hardliners, but it failed. In the months that followed the Soviet Union collapsed and re-formed into what is now known as the Commonwealth of Independent States (CIS), or Russia. Because a crew was aboard *Mir* during this period, many news stories focused on the "plight" of cosmonaut Krikalev, implying that he was "stuck" in space.

During his stay aboard *Mir*, Krikalev participated in six space walks (EVAs) and returned to Earth on 25 March 1992, completing a mission of 311 days. In September 1992 Krikalev attended the annual meeting of the Association of Space Explorers held in Washington, D.C., and was exasperated by the media questions about his being "marooned" in space. Although fluent in English, he felt frustrated in being unable to correct what he thought was a mistaken notion about his extended stay in space.

When the U.S. and Russia agreed on a cooperative program that would lead up to Russia joining in the International Space Station, Sergei Krikalev was one of two cosmonauts chosen to fly on the Shuttle. He flew on Shuttle mission STS-60 in February 1994, and—because of his fluency in English—has assisted in NASA mission control during the early Shuttle/*Mir* rendezvous and docking missions in 1995. He also flew on STS-88, the first assembly flight of the Space Station.

225. Why doesn't NASA build a special rescue spacecraft? What would happen to astronauts on the Space Station if the Shuttle couldn't get up to bring them back? Would they be marooned?

Work is well underway (as of 1999) on the X-38, a crew return vehicle (CRV). The European Space Agency, Germany, and NASA are jointly developing this vehicle. It will be a lightweight spacecraft weighing about 25,000 pounds and be capable of carrying ten astronauts including the crew. Planned to be ready in 2004, it will be docked to the Space Station and be available for emergency use in the event of serious illness or injury, or if an onboard emergency requires the astronauts to abandon the Space Station.

Until it is ready, two Russian Soyuz–type spacecraft will be used for emergency crew return, each capable of bringing three Space Station crew members back to Earth. The X-38 is also being promoted as a space pickup truck. Once in space it can be used to ferry freight between the Space Station and nearby spacecraft.

226. How many launches will it take to get all the pieces of the International Space Station up into orbit? How many pieces (modules) will there be?

Currently (1999), forty-five launches are scheduled (1998–2004) to assemble the Station. This includes twelve Russian launches and thirty-three Shuttle launches. The Station will consist of about twenty major modules and components.

227. How high will the Space Station be above the Earth? Can we see it from the ground? How much of the Earth will the astronauts be able to see? Will they have windows for looking out? How big will it be?

During early stages of assembly the International Space Station will be about 220 miles above the Earth. It will be raised gradually as pieces are added and will be about 270 miles above the Earth when assembly is complete. At this altitude the atmospheric drag is very small but it is enough to require occasional "reboosts" as the altitude drops to around 250 miles. A Russian module on the rear of the station will provide the thrust for the reboost.

At this altitude (250–270 miles) the Space Station astronauts can see about 1,800 miles to the horizon. If you were out on a space walk with a clear view you could see a circular area 3,600 miles across. The Space Station will be at the same altitude as *Skylab* and—although we had the same view—we thought the best view (to see and identify objects best) was within a 550-mile circular region directly below our position. (See Question 153.) The orbital path of the Station will intersect the equator at an angle of 51.6°. This means that the orbit will reach 51.6° north and south latitudes. Approximately 75 percent of the Earth's land surface will lie under the Station's orbital path. If you live within this geographic area you will be able to see it when it flies overhead and weather conditions permit.

The Space Station will have windows in several modules and most will provide a good view of the Earth. One of the modules will have a cupola attached for viewing the outside areas of the station. It will have windows all around and looks a bit like a miniature control tower. It will probably be a very popular place for looking at the Earth.

When fully assembled, the Space Station will be 356 feet wide, 290 feet long, and have over 46,000 cubic feet of internal pressurized volume, (roughly equivalent to the passenger cabin volume of two 747 jetliners). It will have a mass of just under 1,000,000 pounds and will provide living and working space for up to seven astronauts and scientists. The U.S., Europe, Japan, and Russia will have their own modules but scientists onboard will be able to share facilities when conducting investigations or performing experiments.

228. Do the cosmonauts that fly on the Shuttle have to learn English? Do the astronauts that go up to the Russian space station have to learn Russian? Isn't there a risk in having crews that speak different languages?

Cosmonauts flying on the Shuttle have learned English and astronauts flying on the *Mir* space station have learned Russian. In both cases, the cosmonauts and astronauts have trained extensively to be qualified to operate the other nation's spacecraft equipment and also know the limits of their ability. On the Shuttle the astronauts manage the major systems and on the *Mir* Russian space station the cosmonauts do the same. There is always a possibility of miscommunication but all crew members are well-trained on emergency procedures to reduce the probability that language differences could cause a serious problem.

The official language for the International Space Station is English. Crew members on the Space Station will include representatives from the U.S, Canada, Japan, Russia, and eleven members of the European Space Agency (ESA). Participating ESA countries are Belgium, Denmark,

France, Germany, Italy, the Netherlands, Norway, Spain, Sweden, Switzerland, and the United Kingdom.

229. How long will astronauts stay up on the Space Station? What is the advantage of staying up for a long time, say, two years?

At first Space Station crews will be replaced every ninety days. Later the stay time will be extended to 120 days and longer if medical tests and flight experience verify that the crew remain healthy and are able to accomplish their work efficiently. One of the reasons for long stays in space is to develop the experience and knowledge required for long flights to the other planets.

230. Are TV cameras always on you while you're working?

No. For some work, especially in the Spacelab carried by the Shuttle, video cameras are used for hours at a time to record crew activity. For instance, during activation or setup of the Spacelab after launch, cameras are operated to show the ground crew how everything is progressing. The crew operation of experiments may be covered by video to enable ground crews to help if something unusual occurs, or just to have a good visual record of the work done. However, there is no intention to invade the crew's privacy and continuous video recording of crew compartments isn't done.

231. How fast is the Shuttle going when it lands?

About 220 miles per hour. The landing speed may be increased to about 235 miles per hour if it's landing with a heavy payload.

232. How far does it roll after landing?

If depends on the surface wind, the speed at touchdown, and the amount of braking used. Using maximum braking, the Shuttle can stop in about one mile. However, the tires and brakes would have to be replaced after a maximum braking rollout. Normally the rollout distance is under two miles. Over the last few years, drag chutes have been

Space Shuttle *Columbia* The Shuttle is about to land at Edwards Air Force base in 1981, piloted by Astronauts Joe H. Engle and Richard H. Truly. (See Questions 231–236.)

installed on the Shuttles to reduce the landing rollout distance and reduce the wear on the Shuttle brakes.

233. How long does it take for the wheels to come down when the Shuttle is landing?

About six to eight seconds. The landing gear is lowered just before touchdown.

234. How long do the tires last?

They are designed for five normal landings.

235. When the Shuttle is reentering, when does it start to fly like an airplane again?

The aerodynamic control surfaces on the wings begin to be effective at about 250,000 feet altitude and a speed of 26,000 feet per second but the rudder does not become fully effective until the spacecraft has descended to 80,000 feet altitude. From 80,000 feet down to landing, the Shuttle is controlled entirely by the control surfaces.

236. Why do the Shuttle astronauts have to wait so long to get out after landing?

They have to turn off all of the systems of the Shuttle, and they must wait for ground crews to make sure no harmful or toxic gases or fumes are still present in the air around the Shuttle. This takes about thirty minutes to one hour.

237. What causes the toxic gases? Where do the fumes come from?

The toxic gases or fumes are produced in two devices:

1. A gas turbine used to run hydraulic pumps for powering engine gimbals (steering controls), flight controls, and wheel brakes.
2. An evaporator device used to cool equipment as the Shuttle descends below 80,000 feet.

The gas turbine is powered by gas pressure created by decomposing hydrazine, a caustic chemical. The evaporator-cooler uses a mixture of ammonia and water, because the ammonia evaporates more readily for more efficient cooling. An invisible cloud of these gases surrounds the Space Shuttle after landing and must be blown away by special fans used by the ground crews.

238. What happened to the Russian space shuttle? When are they going to fly it again?

The Russian space shuttle, named *Buran* ("snowstorm" or "blizzard") only made one brief (3½ hour) flight into space, unmanned, on 15 November 1988. Because of funding shortages they canceled the program.

239. What caused the power blackout on the Russian _Mir_ space station? What can we do to prevent the same thing from happening on the new (International) Space Station?

On October 12, 1994, power system sensors on the _Mir_ space station detected a low level of battery charge and automatically shut off all power, plunging the station into darkness. This was what the system was designed to do and the incident was caused by unintentional excessive power consumption. The cosmonauts used flashlights to move batteries around and then used their Soyuz spacecraft engines to maneuver the station to aim the _Mir_'s solar arrays to face the sun for battery recharge

Following this incident a strict schedule of power use was instituted and the problem has not happened again. A careful schedule of power use is planned for the International Space Station to avoid a similar occurrence and ground monitoring (mission control) should provide advanced warning of any approaching problem.

240. What kind of things would we want to build in space?

In addition to the International Space Station, some of the structures being considered are:

1. Large communication antennas: eventually most phone and television links will be through space relay units.
2. Solar power stations: solar energy collectors and transmitters.
3. Laboratories and manufacturing facilities serving specialized needs (basic research in materials science and biology).
4. Space materials processing and manufacturing (factories).
5. Storage warehouses.
6. Large spacecraft-assembly facilities in Earth orbit—for future space missions to the moon or Mars, for example.
7. Refueling and repair depots.
8. Medical research facilities.

9. A lunar base.
10. A Mars base.
11. The construction of space colonies that would be populated by thousands of people have been proposed, but this will be far into the future.

Many of these facilities can be combined and the Space Station is an example. It includes facilities 3, 4, and 8 listed previously. Some will function independently once assembled unless they require repair and be tended through telerobotic systems managed by operators on Earth. Large antennas and the solar power station are examples of independent facilities. Some would be operated remotely from the ground and be visited periodically for servicing. A space materials processing and manufacturing factory is an example of a remotely operated production unit.

241. Why is the launch center located in Florida?

The air force selected Cape Canaveral for missile testing in the 1950s, and when NASA was formed in 1958, it relied on air force experience and facilities to assist in the launches of the early spacecraft. Mercury and Gemini orbital space missions were launched by air force boosters (rockets) originally designed for missiles. During the 1960s, NASA developed its own launch facilities on Cape Canaveral at the Kennedy Space Center. These facilities have evolved into a highly reliable launch base for manned and unmanned spacecraft.

The air force chose the Florida location because of several favorable features of the site:

1. The secluded location simplified security.
2. The site faced the Atlantic Ocean — rockets could be launched eastward over the ocean without risk to the general population.
3. Rail, highway, air, and water transportation were reasonably accessible.
4. The mild subtropical climate provided moderate weather for year-round operations.

FLORIDA LOCATIONS HAVE FAVORABLE FEATURES

5. A southerly location in the United States makes best use of the "slingshot" effect caused by the Earth's rotation. The eastward motion of the Earth's surface because of its rotation adds over 1,000 MPH to the speed of a rocket launched in an easterly direction at the equator. This advantage decreases progressively as the launch site is moved north or south of the equator. Thus, a launch site in the southern part of the continental United States

would be best. At Cape Canaveral, the eastward surface velocity is almost 900 MPH, a distinct asset for orbital launches.

Note: For space vehicles that orbit north-south and go over the North and South Poles, a near-equatorial launch-site location provides no advantage. The main consideration for such launch sites is to have an uninhabited area north or south of the launch site so that launch failures pose no threat to people below the path of the rocket. U.S. military polar reconnaissance spacecraft are launched in a southerly direction from a launch site in California (Vandenberg Launch Site), located about fifty miles west of Santa Barbara.

242. How has medical care benefited from the space program?

Medical and health care techniques have profited immensely from space technology. Automated patient monitoring, a wide range of diagnostic tools and techniques, artificial limbs with much greater capability, microsurgery techniques and equipment, improved quality of X-ray interpretation are capabilities or improvements that are indebted to space research in whole or in part.

243. What are the benefits and advantages of being able to make direct visual observations of the Earth from space?

I discovered a branch of the New Zealand current near the Chatham Islands in the southwest Pacific Ocean. This was important because it was a new fishing area. Currents carry plankton, which is the base of the ocean food chain (the "bread of the sea"). Small organisms are eaten by larger ones and this process continues until commercial food fish are present.

Our crew was the first to receive formalized training to make systematic visual observations for specific applications. Although our training was limited, it did give us a good idea of what information the scientists wanted. We observed the growth cycle of crops in Australia and Argentina, structural (geologic) fault lines in many areas, weather effects, ocean surface features, erupting volcanoes, and we studied several desert and arid areas.

Based upon observations of the Sahel, a broad region spanning the continent of Africa south of the Sahara Desert, I theorized that enormous quantities of dust were being carried high into the atmosphere and far out to the sea. Six months later, a series of weather satellite pictures were used to observe the movement of a dust cloud from Africa all the way to the Caribbean Sea. This was significant because the amount of dust in the air may affect cloud formation and rainfall. In fact, after this particular dust cloud reached the Caribbean, later satellite pictures showed a large area of clouds covering the same area as the dust cloud.

In 1998 scientists discovered that industrial pollution and dust are carried by winds from China and central Asia across the Pacific ocean and the Western U.S. all the way to Texas. In this case, the pollution remained concentrated enough to cause a local increase to two-thirds the federal health standard limit. The pollution from Asia was tracked by satellite and was observed to reach the U.S. in less than a week.

244. How many different kinds of satellites do we have?

We're all familiar with the weather and communications satellites because of their applications to television. Weather satellites save billions of dollars and thousands of lives each year by providing advance warning of approaching storm systems. Communications satellites provide immediate and worldwide television coverage of political, social, and entertainment events from any place on the globe. Communication satellites are also being used to locate downed aircraft by zeroing in on emergency-location beacons onboard the plane. Some pager systems use satellites for relay and a satellite system is now in place to handle personal telephone calls. Many more satellite phone relay systems are scheduled to become operational after the year 2000. These satellite phone systems will have very few "blind spots" and will cover the entire world. The air force's Global Positioning System (GPS) is a satellite system that provides very accurate location of your position on Earth and in space. (See Question 246.) A cooperative satellite system (U.S. and Russian combination) can locate the position of ships in distress or downed aircraft when an emergency beacon is activated. The system relays this information to Earth to aid in rescue operations. Imaging satellites provide pictures of the entire Earth and have almost unlimited application. They can be used to estimate agricultural yields (by type of crop), identify agricultural and ranching areas that are being misused (soil depletion or overgrazing), conduct forest inventories (and identify unhealthy/diseased trees), assess environmental changes, identify pollution sources, construct better maps, identify potential mineral deposits, determine population distribution, locate icebergs and ice jams (for shipping safety), identify geologic faults, detect underground water sources, track the distribution of ash from volcano eruptions, and so forth.

Scientific satellites have added enormously to our knowledge of the sun and planets of our solar system and the universe as a whole. The immediate practical application of such studies may not be obvious but the payoff is real. Studies of the sun and the solar system atmosphere enable us to improve communications here on Earth. Scientists are eager to begin studies of the planet Venus because it is considered a "twin" of the Earth. However, its atmosphere creates a greenhouse effect that keeps the surface of the planet hot enough to melt lead (over 800° Fahrenheit). We are concerned that the Earth is gradually developing a similar effect owing to increasing amounts of carbon dioxide in our atmosphere. Venus provides a real laboratory to learn more about this process to enable better understanding of what is happening to our own atmosphere.

245. What will the astronauts do on the Space Station?

The Space Station's major areas of research and objectives for these investigations are:

1. Life sciences: Develop the knowledge and techniques to enable people to spend longer time in space without health penalties and use this knowledge to improve health care for us here on Earth.
2. Earth sciences: Assess global trends in atmospheric quality, weather, climate change, vegetation and land use, mineral and food resources, and the health of fresh water and the oceans.

3. Space science: Explore the solar system, understand better sun-Earth relationships, study the structure and evolution of the universe, and look for planets around other stars where life could originate.
4. Microgravity science: Exploit very-low gravity conditions to study atomic/molecular structures (both in manufacturing materials and biological samples), combustion science (more efficient furnace burners reduce pollution and save fuel), materials science (better electronic devices and even artificial bones), and fundamental physics (testing of theories that apply to topics ranging from weather prediction to astronomy).
5. Engineering research: Development of new technologies that have application to communications (better phones and computers), air and water quality improvement, lower construction cost for houses and buildings, and improved automated manufacturing processes.
6. Space product development: Discovery of space manufactured products that are the basis for the creation of new industries for the commercial and industrial community. One such product would be new medicines or pharmaceuticals.

246. In addition to the International Space Station, what other international cooperative programs are being pursued?

During the decades of the 1980s and 1990s, space exploration and practical applications of space satellites have grown to include a much broader representation from nations around the globe. The European Space Agency (ESA), the Japanese space agency (NASDA), and the People's Republic of China all now have their own launch capability for the spacecraft that serve their needs. In addition, many countries operate their own satellites launched by other countries and subscribe to satellite services provided by other nations' spacecraft. U.S. satellites have been launched by the Chinese, U.S. experiments have been flown on Russian missions, and we have launched a number of satellites for other countries. A U.S. company will provide and maintain a satellite phone system for a large area of the Mideast and part of Africa. A satellite phone system is an effective solution for sparsely populated geographic regions where the installation of telephone land lines would be too expensive. The goals of the U.S. and Russia have also become focused on a range of activities with strong mutual interest. Both countries, and the Europeans as well, have Earth satellite systems to monitor and evaluate the environment above and on the Earth. The Global Positioning System is being used worldwide by aircraft, ships at sea, trucking companies, and individuals (hunters and hikers). Cars can now have a GPS receiver installed that can determine the car's location within tens of feet and display its position on a map showing its position on city streets or an interstate highway system. In addition to geographic location the GPS can determine the car's speed and elevation above sea level. The Space Station will use a more accurate mode of the GPS to calculate the position and attitude of the assembly as it orbits the Earth. *Attitude* of the Station is the way it's pointed and tilted relative to a reference such as the Earth's horizon. This information is needed to assure the large solar arrays are facing the sun, for example. The GPS service is free and some receivers can be bought for a few hundred dollars.

The exploration of the solar system is another major area of mutual interest. This includes a wide variety of scientific satellites and will grow to include manned exploration as well. Manned missions to the moon, the establishment of a moon base, exploratory manned missions to Mars and constructing a base on Mars are efforts that could benefit from full international participation. Fortunately, there has been healthy international cooperation in sharing information of purely scientific nature. The problems or impediments to cooperation usually occur when the products or benefits of a given space effort are deemed to provide a military, marketing, or commercial advantage to the one performing the venture.

NASA's Shuttle program has cultivated strong international cooperation through the *Spacelab* project and by flying astronauts from several other countries. The *Spacelab* was built by the European Space Agency (ESA) and is flown aboard the Shuttle. ESA participants in the

Spacelab program include ten European countries and fifty industrial firms.

The Russian guest cosmonaut program has included space flights for representatives from over ten other countries. The international Space Station will include modules from the U.S., Russia, Japan, and ESA as major elements of the Space Station assembly. The Canadians will provide the robot arm for the Space Station. There is a strong commonality of goals and a healthy move toward increasing cooperation among the nations pursuing space exploration and applications. Differences and rivalries will remain, but they are gradually taking the form of commercial and business competition rather than military challenge.

247. What do you think is the greatest contribution of the space program?

I believe the most important contribution is the subtle and intangible benefits that have occurred within the minds and spirits of people. On the large scale, the instant communication between peoples across the globe has been the single most important instrument of social and political change we've ever seen. This is directly attributable to the communications satellites and live television relay capability. Free access to information and news is the first step in the march toward freedom of individual thought and action (where it does not already exist).

The revolt against repressive governments and leaders in Eastern Europe was fueled by the knowledge that such repression was not the way it had to be. Incidentally, the first action by a rebelling population is to seize control of the television stations to get their message to their own countrymen, and also to the rest of the world (via satellite). Where repression still exists, access to news and information is rigidly controlled.

On an individual basis the benefits are aroused curiosity, the intellectual stimulation that attends exploration, an appreciation of the importance of goals, the virtue of dedication, the necessity of commitment, and belief in one's ability to accomplish. The overall attitudes of people influence their aspirations and ability to attain.

Awareness of the achievability of difficult goals has a strong influence on the objectives we set for ourselves. I believe the most beneficial legacy of the space program has been to elevate our expectation of ourselves.

Appendix

1. SUMMARY OF PHYSIOLOGICAL EFFECTS
2. GUIDE TO INFORMATION AND RESOURCES
3. TABLE: RESOURCE GUIDE BY STATE OF RESIDENCY
4. WEB ADDRESSES
5. SPACE CAMPS
6. SPACE-RELATED ORGANIZATIONS
7. RECOMMENDED READING AND OTHER REFERENCES
8. CATALOGS
9. ABBREVIATIONS

1. Summary of Physiological Effects

Feelings, Sensations

The following feelings or symptoms may be experienced by crew members. Note: An individual crew member will not necessarily experience all of these effects. Many never get sick or have headaches. Also, the degree or extent to which astronauts feel these effects will vary from person to person.

- Giddy, light-headed feeling.
- Bug-eyed sensation.
- "Flush" feeling in face.
- Awareness of neck pulse; throbbing in head.
- Hypersensitivity to head movements; excessive or exaggerated sensation of rotation caused by head movements.
- Moderate to severe headache.
- Space sickness—nausea, vomiting.
- Reluctance to belch; risk of regurgitation; excessive flatus owing to gas retention (gas retention problem may be less for Shuttle—cabin pressure is higher).
- Head stuffiness; nasal, sinus or ear congestion. Head congestion is relieved by exercise and, to some extent, by eating.
- Lower backache; experienced by many crew members—gradually disappears after 10–15 days.
- "Head nod" during sleep (probably caused by carotid pulse); causes mild nausea in some crew members.

- Inverse "déjà vu"; surroundings appear unfamiliar when viewed from unusual perspective; immediately corrected by assuming a familiar body (head-eye) position relative to the physical environment (work area).
- Light flashes "seen" by dark-adapted crew members when passing through low spots or regions in the Earth's radiation belts, polar regions or while traveling through deep space beyond the Earth's trapped radiation zones. Three explanations have been proposed to explain the light flashes seen by crew members. They are:

A. Cerenkov radiation (emission of photons by particles slowed by fluid in the eye).
B. Light generated by particles ionizing fluid in the eye.
C. Artificial light stimulus caused by particles impacting retinal sensors in the eye.

- Tissue drying; chapped hands and lips, dryness in the eyes (eye irritation or sensitivity). This lasts about one week.
- Peculiar soft or puffy texture/feeling in the mouth, sometimes described as *cotton fuzz* feeling probably owed to the low pressure inside *Skylab* (one-third of the pressure used in the Shuttle).
- Noticeable changes in sense of taste and smell—pattern varies with individual. Most astronauts exhibit a preference for greater use of condiments during space flights.
- Ambient spacecraft noise: Noise from fans, pumps, and radio transmissions can be distracting and may affect a crew member's ability to concentrate or go to sleep.

Appearance, Posture/Muscular Changes

The following changes affect the outward appearance of individuals.

- Distended/swollen veins in forehead and neck.
- Facial edema; puffiness in face; bags under eyes. Moderate decrease in edema after 3–4 days.

- Decreased girth measurements of thighs and calves of legs owed to lowered volume of blood and tissue fluids in the legs (bird legs).
- Facial tissue float or rise; high cheekbone appearance combined with a slight eye-squinting effect.
- Internal organs shift upward, creating a "wasp waist" appearance and possibly a reduced vital capacity or inability to breathe as deeply as on Earth. Waist measurement is approximately three inches less for crew members of average size.
- Hair float (long hair).
- Relaxed body posture is semierect, knees bent slightly, upper back curled slightly forward, loss of curvature in small of back; arms float upward at chest height, shoulders rise up in a "shrug" position.
- Spinal lengthening and straightening causes increase in body length (height) of approximately two inches.

Performance, Endurance

An astronaut's ability to execute tasks may be influenced (degraded or improved) by the following factors.

- Inability or difficulty in bending forward or in assuming a seated position; seat belt required to hold body seated in chair. Easier to bend forward after several weeks.
- Loss (atrophy) of muscle mass and tone in the large muscles of the legs. Partially arrested by exercise during flight. Rapid recovery after return. Main cause is inability to achieve the normal workload stress present on Earth. Contributes to decreased girth measurements of thighs and calves.
- *Space crud*—a general malaise or "down" feeling that occurs 3–4 hours after eating; similar to onset of flu or a cold. Quickly relieved by eating.
- Eyeglasses may tend to bob up and down or fly off during rapid head turns if earpieces don't fit properly or if the glasses don't have retention bands or straps.

- Persistent tendency to throw objects too high when tossing items (apparently allowing for nonexistent gravity drop).
- No significant change in motor skills or coordination tasks.
- Enhanced clarity of vision of objects viewed in space vacuum. This ability to see with increased sharpness has led some to describe such views as *gemlike* or *unreal in clarity*. Generally considered to be owed to absence of light scattering in vacuum.
- Ability to see 10–20 percent more stars.
- Visual scene orientation prejudice; predisposition and preference to view scenes as one is accustomed to seeing them (even though there is no sensed direction of gravity). Crew member will move to orient "eye plane" to achieve the preferred scene orientation (until it looks "right side up").
- Handling large (Earth-heavy) objects is much simpler and easier in weightlessness, though manipulating tiny objects is more difficult because of a tendency to overcontrol or flick or knock them about.

Other Effects, Including Postflight

Other effects noticed during and following space flight include the following:

- Reduced total blood volume; Prolonged cessation of red cell production with eventual stabilized total red cell population commensurate with the reduced blood volume (long flights). Postflight anemia (long flights).
- Bone mass loss or bone demineralization occurs during space flight (extent of loss varies with the individual). Soviet flight results on long missions indicate the bone mass loss can be controlled by exercise regimens.
- Lingering (surrounding) body odor may occur if crew member is in an area where fan circulation is poor. There is no convective circulation in weightlessness.
- During heavy exercise, auxiliary fan circulation may be required to prevent overheating; sweat pooling or accumulation on the

body can be a problem (inadvertently release of sweat globs into the air).

- Radiation tissue damage (extent unknown). Radiation dosage increases with time spent in space and is currently considered to be a career-limiting consideration.
- Slight changes in proportionate time spent at various levels of sleep. Also, sleep requirement appears to be 1–2 hours less (per day) for crew members while in space.
- Post-light anemia. Readjustment is rapid as body restores red cell population to match the normal blood volume for 1-g Earth conditions.
- Perception of magnitude of heft and weight forces (postflight).

  - Objects feel heavier.
  - External body pressure sensations owed to sitting, lying (particularly when rolling on one's side) feel unnaturally excessive.
  - Exaggerated perceptions disappear within a week of return.

- Muscle/tendon/joint soreness (postflight).

  - Lower back and calf muscle soreness (1–2 weeks).
  - Achilles tendon soreness/ache (2 weeks — 1 month).
  - Knee-joint soreness during long-distance running. Joint problems may persist for several months.

- Standing/walking difficulties (postflight).

  - Faintness upon standing up (orthostatic intolerance).
  - Unsteadiness
  - Readaptation (correction) is rapid.

2. Guide to Information and Resources

Items 1–9 list general educational space-related materials available from NASA. Educators, teachers, and students should write, explaining your need or requirement, to the *first* address serving your state in the Table below. Internet and Web addresses are also listed for some services.

1. NASA *Teacher Resource Centers* contain a wealth of information for educators: publications, reference books, slides, audio cassettes, video cassettes, telelecture programs, computer programs, lesson plans and activities, and lists of publications available from government and non-government sources.

Write to the *second* address serving your state in the Table below, providing the following information with your request:

> Your position/title (name optional)
> Name of school or institution and mailing address
> Level of material: elementary, junior high, high school, college, or other (specify)
> Subject Interest:
>
> > Sciences: life, earth, physical, mathematics, astronomy, aeronautics
> > Other: humanities or specify

2. *Central Operation of Resources for Educators* (CORE) is a NASA centralized mail-order audiovisual library for educators; no printed ma-

terials are available. Submit a written request on your school letterhead for a catalog and order forms. Orders are processed for a small fee that includes the cost of the media.

NASA CORE
Lorain County Joint Vocational School
15181 Route 58 South
Oberlin, OH 44074
Phone: (216) 774-1051 Ext.293 or 294

3. *Aerospace Education Services Program* (AESP) specialists conduct workshops for teachers each summer at NASA field centers, elementary and secondary schools, and on college campuses. Workshops cover astronomy, aeronautics, life in space, principles of rocketry, Earth science, and remote sensing. A typical workshop includes how-to and hands-on activities to help teachers incorporate what they learn into classroom activities and programs to supplement existing curricula. Contact the Center Education Programs Officer at the NASA field center that serves the school's geographic area (Table), or contact:

Elementary and Secondary Programs Branch
Educational Affairs Division
Code XEE, NASA Headquarters
Washington, DC 20546
(202) 453-8386 or Website at http://www.okstate.edu.aesp/
AESP.html

4. *NASA Education Homepage* provides current information and instructional resource materials to teachers, faculty, and students. A wide range of information is available, including science, mathematics, engineering and technology lesson plans, historical information related to aeronautics and space programs, current status reports on NASA projects, news releases, information on NASA educational programs, and useful software and graphics files. Go to these resources through the NASA Education homepage at: http://www.hq.nasa.gov/office/codef/education

5. *NASA Spacelink* has been developed specifically for use by the educational community. An electronic library, Spacelink not only provides information on NASA projects but also teacher guides, pictures, and computer software to enhance classroom instruction. Spacelink also provides links to other NASA resources on the Internet and may be accessed at: http://spacelink.msfc.nasa.gov For additional information or to ask a question, E-mail a message to: comments@spacelink. msfc.nasa.gov

6. The *University Programs Branch* at each NASA field center (Table 1) conducts a variety of programs for university students and faculty and serves as a focal point for information about research, grant, and fellowship opportunities as well as other university-related activity at the center. This office awards fellowships to graduate students whose research interests are compatible with NASA programs. About 120 new awardees are selected each year on a competitive basis. For information about the University Programs Branch at NASA Headquarters, contact:

> University Programs Branch
> Code XEU, NASA Headquarters
> Washington, DC 20546
> (202) 453-8344

7. Statellite Videoconferences—During the school year, a series of educational programs is delivered by satellite to teachers across the country. The content of each videoconference varies, but all cover aeronautics or space science topics of interest to the educational community. The broadcasts are interactive; a number is flashed across the bottom of the screen, and viewers can call collect to ask questions or take part in a discussion. For further information, contact:

> Educational Technology Branch
> Educational Affairs Division
> Code XE
> NASA Headquarters

Washington, DC 20546
(202) 453-8388

or

Videoconference Coordinator
NASA Aerospace Education Services Program
Oklahoma State University
300 N. Cordell
Stillwater, OK 74078
(405) 744-7015 or Website at http://www.okstate.edu/aesp/vc.html

This Internet site provides the capability to register your school for videoconferences, contains the current schedule of videoconferences, and posts a current schedule of NASA video programming.

8. NASA Cooperative Educational Program—The Cooperative Educational Program gives high school, college, and graduate students an opportunity to work at a field center while completing their education. Each field center negotiates its own cooperative agreements with schools in its area. Contact the Center Personnel Officer at the NASA field center serving your area (Table), or contact:

Personnel Policy and Work Force Effectiveness Division
Mail Code NPM, NASA Headquarters
Washington, DC 20546
(202) 453-2603

9. *NASA Select Television*—If you or your school cable TV system carries NASA Select or has a satellite antenna, NASA Select programs may be received and videotaped. The programs are public domain; they can be taped, dubbed (copied), and used repeatedly without copyright infringement. NASA Select transmits live and taped programs. This includes live and playback coverage of Shuttle missions in progress as well as a variety of educational programs. The educational

and historical programming is aimed at inspiring students to achieve, especially in mathematics, science, and technology. NASA Select is transmitted from channel 9 of the S2 satellite (Spacenet 2, transponder 9). For satellite antenna reception tune to S2, channel 9 at 69 degrees west with horizontal polarization, frequency 3880.0 megahertz, audio on 6.8 megahertz. NASA also transmits on channel 5 occasionally. *A schedule for NASA Select is published daily on NASA Spacelink.* See paragraph 5 for Spacelink Web and Internet addresses. For more information on NASA Select, contact:

> NASA Select
> NASA Headquarters
> Code P
> Washington, DC 20546

The following organizations are not directly related to NASA but provide various forms of assistance for educators and students.

10. *Challenger Center for Space Science Education*—Students and Teachers: Grades 5–8. The *Challenger* Center is an educational organization that strives through innovative teaching and learning experiences to inspire and prepare students for the technological demands of the future. Programs include workshops for teachers and learning centers for students. A key feature of the learning centers is a Space Life Mission Simulator that provides students with an opportunity to participate in simulated missions with future-oriented themes. The Center is building a library of mission scenarios to provide a wide variety of exciting mission simulations.

Learning Centers are funded locally through a variety of approaches ranging from local governments to industry sponsorship. The *Challenger* Center is a private group but works closely with regional NASA facilities. *Challenger* Center was begun as a memorial to the seven astronauts who died in the *Challenger* disaster.

> *Challenger* Center for Space Science Education
> Suite 190, 1101 King Street

Alexandria, VA 22314
(703) 683-9740 or Website at http://www.challenger.org

11. *The National Air and Space Museum's Educational Resource Center*—Teachers: K–12. The Educational Resource Center provides lesson plans, filmstrips, slide sets, videotapes, computer software (public domain and commercial), and periodicals. The Center also provides ordering information for these products. Teachers should write or call, specifying grade level and topic.

Educational Resource Center
Office of Education P-700
National Air and Space Museum
Smithsonian Institution
Washington, DC 20560
(202) 786-2106 or Website at http://www.nasm.si.edu

3. TABLE

Select your state or geographic area from this column.	Students: Write to the first address listed for your area explaining your need. Educators: Write to the second address listed for your area. Also, you may Fax or visit the Website, if one is listed for your area.
Alaska Arizona California Hawaii Idaho Montana Nevada Oregon Utah Washington Wyoming	Chief, Educational Programs Branch Mail Stop 204-12 NASA Ames Research Center Moffet Field, CA 94035-1000 or NASA Ames Research Center Educator Resource Center, MS 253-2 Moffet Field, CA 94035-1000 Phone: (650) 604-3574 Fax: (650) 604-3445 http://ccf.arc.nasa.gov/dx/basket/trc/trchome.html
California cities near the Dryden Flight Research Center (Edwards Air Force Base)	NASA Dryden Flight Research Center 45108 North Third Street East Lancaster, CA 93535 Phone: (805) 948-7347 Fax: (805) 948-7068 http://www.dfrc.nasa.gov/trc.html

Table   **195**

Southern California	NASA Jet Propulsion Laboratory
	Mail Stop CS-530
	4800 Oak Grove Drive
	Pasadena, CA 91109
	Phone: (818) 354-6916
	Fax: (818) 354-8080
	http://learn.jpl.nasa.gov
Connecticut	Chief, Education Office, Code 130
Delaware	NASA Goddard Space Flight Center
District of Columbia	Greenbelt, MD 20771-0001
Maine	or
Maryland	NASA Goddard Space Flight Center
Massachusetts	Educator Resources Laboratory, MC 130.3
New Hampshire	Greenbelt, MD 20771-1000
New Jersey	Phone: (301) 286-8570
New York	Fax: (301) 286-1781
Pennsylvania	http://pao.gsfc.nasa.gov/gsfc/edu/trl/
Rhode Island	welcome.html
Vermont	
Colorado	Education and Information Services
Kansas	Branch AP-2
Nebraska	NASA Johnson Space Center
New Mexico	2101 NASA Road One
North Dakota	Houston, TX 77058-3696
Oklahoma	or
South Dakota	NASA Johnson Space Center
Texas	Space Center Houston
	1601 NASA Road One
	Houston, TX 77058
	Phone: (281) 244-2129
	Fax: (281) 483-9638
	http://www.jsc.nasa.gov

Florida Georgia Puerto Rico Virgin Islands	Chief, Education and Services Branch Mail Code PA-ESB NASA Kennedy Space Center Kennedy Space Center, FL 32899-0001 or NASA John F. Kennedy Space Center Educator Resources Laboratory Mail Code ERC Kennedy Space Center, FL 32999-0001 Phone: (407) 867-4090 Fax (407) 867-7242
Kentucky North Carolina South Carolina Virginia West Virginia	Center Education Program Officer MS 400 NASA Langley Research Center Hampton, VA 23681-0001 Phone: (757) 864-3313 or Virginia Air and Space Center NASA Teacher Resource Center 600 Settler's Landing Road Hampton, VA 23669-4033 Phone: (757) 727-0900, Ext. 757 Fax: (757) 727-0898 http://www.vasc.org/erc
Virginia's and Maryland's eastern shores	Wallops Flight Facility Visitor Center, Bldg. J-17 Wallops Island, VA 23337-5099 Phone: (757) 824-2298 Fax: (757) 824-1776

Table **197**

Illinois Indiana Michigan Minnesota Ohio Wisconsin	Chief, Office of Educational Programs NASA Glenn Research Center 21000 Brookpark Road, MS 7-4 Cleveland, OH 44135-3191 or NASA Glenn Research Center Educator Resource Center 21000 Brookpark Road, MS 8-1 Cleveland, OH 44135-3191 Phone: (216) 433-2017 Fax: (216) 433-3601
Alabama Arkansas Iowa Louisiana Missouri Tennessee	Precollege Officer, Mail Stop C 060 NASA Marshall Space Flight Center Huntsville, AL 35812-0001 Phone: (256) 544-8811 or U.S. Space and Rocket Center NASA Educator Resource Center One Tranquility Base Huntsville, AL 35758 Phone: (256) 544-5812 Fax: (256) 544-5820 http://www.msfc.nasa.gov/education/erc
Mississippi	Manager, Educational Programs Mail Stop MA00 NASA John C. Stennis Space Center Stennis Space Center, MS 39529-6000 or NASA Stennis Space Center Educator Resource Center Building 1200 Stennis Space Center, MS 39529-6000 Phone: (601) 688-3337 Fax: (601) 688-2824

4. WEB ADDRESSES

Current Events/News/Current Programs

Today @ NASA: Provides the latest NASA news. This site also has newsworthy imagery such as the latest views from the Hubble Space Telescope.
   http://www.hq.nasa.gov/office/pao/newsroom/today.html

NASA Newsroom: Latest on NASA, including biographies.
   http://www.nasa.gov/hqpao/newsroom.html

Space News Roundup: NASA JSC weekly publication; daily information is also available.
   http://www.jsc.nasa.gov/pao/roundup/weekly
   http://www.jsc.nasa.gov/pao/roundup   (daily)

Florida Today Space Online: Space news and information.
   http://www.flatoday.com/space/today/index.html

Shuttle Web: Provides information on upcoming Shuttle missions.
   http://Shuttle.nasa.gov

Shuttle Mission Guide: Provides information on Shuttle missions.
   http://www.ksc.nasa.gov/Shuttle/missions/missions.html

International Space Station: Latest ISS news, assembly flights plus pictures and many links to other ISS topics.
   http://station.nasa.gov

Space Telescope Science Institute: Provides a wealth of information related to the Hubble Space Telescope.
http://www.stsci.edu

Johnson Space Center (JSC) Homepage: This site has links to a wide range of topics.
http://www.jsc.nasa.gov

Kennedy Space Center (KSC) Homepage: This site has links to a wide range of topics including how to get a pass to watch a Shuttle launch.
http://www.ksc.nasa.gov

Education Focus

NASA Education Homepage: Gateway to information regarding NASA educational programs and services for educators and students.
http://www.hq.nasa.gov/education

NASA Education Program Homepage:
http://www.hq.nasa.gov/office/codef/education/index.html

NASA Learning Technologies Project (LTP): Online resources and activities for the classroom.
http://learn.ivv.nasa.gov (LTP homepage)

Challenger *Center*: Classroom educational materials, suggestions for projects, and much more.
http://www.challenger.org

NASA Classroom of the Future (COTF): Has the mission to improve K–12 mathematics, science, and technology education.
http://www.cotf.edu

NASA Johnson Space Center: Resource materials on Space Station, Shuttle launch schedule, Shuttle mission highlights, NASA historical documents, NASA fact sheets. Can be reached through the JSC home-page or directly at the following Website.

http:www.jsc.nasa.gov/pao/educators

NASA Spacelink: Provides educational materials (Item 6 under "Guide To Information and Resources"). Join the "SpaceLink EXPRESS" (on-line) and receive E-mail announcements of new educational materials.

http://spacelink.nasa.gov

http://spacelink.nasa.gov/products (NASA educational products)

http://spacelink.nasa.gov/xh/express.html (Join Spacelink EXPRESS and receive E-mail.)

http://spacelink.nasa.gov/.index.html (Astronaut selection and train-ing plus many other topics)

NASA's K–12 Internetinitiative: Provides support and services for schools, teachers, and students to fully use the Internet as a basic tool for learning.

http://quest.arc.nasa.gov

Aerospace Education Services Program (*AESP*): Specialists conduct workshops for teachers each summer at NASA field centers, elementary and secondary schools, and on college campuses.

http://www.okstate.edu.aesp/AESP.html

Astronaut Focus

Astronaut Biographies:

http://www.jsc.nasa.gov/Bios/astrobio.html

Astronaut Fact Book: Lists astronauts by selection group, colleges at-tended by astronauts, and lists all U.S. space flights to date. The fol-lowing site can also be reached through the JSC homepage.

http://www.jsc.nasa.gov/pao/factsheets/nasapubs/9703008.doc

Astronaut Selection: Can be reached through the JSC homepage or directly at the following site.
http://38.201.67.70/shuttle/reference/faq/astronaut.html

Space Imagery/Pictures/Movies

Space Movie Archive: Computer animations from space missions and science fiction.
http://graffiti.u-bordeaux.fr/MAPBX/roussel/astro.html

SEDS: Provides an excellent image collection.
http://seds.lpl.arizona.edu

Other imagery is available from links on NASA Websites.

Solar System

Welcome To The Planets: (NASA) Includes a listing of all missions to the planets.
http://pds.jpl.nasa.gov/planets

Earth's Moon Focus:
Moon Link (Access to other sites):
http://www.moonlink.com
Lunar Geology Class (by Astronaut Harrison Schmitt):
http://elvis.neep.wisc.edu/~neep602/neep602.html

Mars: Links to far-out topics plus serious analyses.
http://personalwebs.myriad.net/tgunn

Jupiter: Images, animation, statistics, and section on impact of comet with the giant planet.
http://www.astro.cz/solar/eng/jupiter.html

Solar System Simulator: Designed for trajectory analysis at the Jet Propulsion Laboratory, this site also lets you view planets from the vantage point of other bodies.
   http://space.jpl.nasa.gov/history.html

Space Programs/Projects

Skylab: America's first space station.
   http://station.nasa.gov/reference/history/skylab.index.html
   http://www.ksc.nasa.gov/history/skylab.html

Shuttle/Mir *Program*: Covers nine dockings and seven astronaut stays aboard *Mir*. Two NASA sites.
   http://shuttle-mir.nasa.gov
   http://www.hq.nasa.gov.osf/mir

Shuttle Missions:
   http://www.ksc.nasa.gov/search/htdig

Shuttle Launches:
   http://www.ksc.gov/shuttle/missions/missions.html

Office of Space Flight (OSF) Shuttle Page (NASA Headquarters):
   http://www.hq.nasa.gov/osf/shuttle

General Reference

SkyNet: Astronomy and space information—good starting point for school reports.
   http://pages.prodigy.com/SkyNet

NASA History Office:
   http://www.hq.nasa.gov/office/pao/History/history/html

National Space Society Online: Ask an astronaut a question (online) and see the answer displayed.
   http://www.nss.org

The Planetary Society: In addition to the Website you may select an E-mail option and you'll be transferred to an E-mail page where you can ask questions.
　http://planetary.org
　If not at Website, E-mail questions to:
　tps@mars.planetary.org

Smithsonian National Air and Space Museum: Lists new exhibits, explains how to plan a visit for groups (general public and students) and provides a form to print, fill out, and mail in or FAX to making reservations.
　http://www.nasm.si.edu

National Space Science Data Center (space history):
　http://nssdc.gsfc.nasa.gov

5. Space Camps

Although NASA works closely with U.S. Space Camp and other organizations that provide youth and adult space-related activities and training programs, they are not run by NASA. The following is a list of groups that offer space camp–type activities. For additional information, contact the organization directly.

U.S. Space and Rocket Center/U.S. Space Camp

U.S. Space Camp has camps in Huntsville, Alabama, Titusville, Florida, and Mountain View, California in the U.S, and Japan and Belgium. Camps are planned for England and Italy. Contact the Space and Rocket Center for details.

One Tranquility Base
Huntsville, AL 35807-0680
(800) 468-7022 and Website: http://www.spacecamp.com

The Space and Rocket Center provides a wide range of activities:

U.S. Space Camp
Grades: 4, 5, 6, 7
five-day program

U.S. Space Academy, Level I
Grades: 8, 9, 10
ten-day program

U.S. Space Academy, Level II
Grades: 11, 12, freshman
ten-day college accredited program

U.S. Space Academy/Adult Programs I and II
Ages: Adult
three-day program
ten-day program also available

Future Astronaut Training Program

Kansas Cosmosphere and Space Center
1100 N. Plum
Hutchinson, KS 67501
(316) 662-2305 and Website: www.cosmo.org

Grades: 7,8,9, and 10
five-day program during summer

Shuttle Camp

Space Center
Education Office
P.O. Box 533
Alamogordo, NM 88311-0533
(800) 545-4021
(505) 437-2840, Ext. 29 or 23, and Website: http://www.zianet/space

Mercury: Grades 3–4, half-day program
Gemini: Grades 5–6, full-day program
Apollo: Grades 7–9, full-day program

6. Space-Related Organizations

The following organizations provide a wide variety of services and activities to aid the public in learning more about space exploration and space topics. Some cater to specific age groups or are limited to educational professionals. The target group is indicated for each organization.

Young Astronaut Council
(Elementary and Junior High School Students)

The Young Astronaut Council (YAC) is not a part of NASA; it is a private organization. For information on YAC and the Young Astronaut Program you should contact the Young Astronaut Council directly to receive additional information and to find out if there is a YAC chapter in your area.

YAC was established to guide the Young Astronaut Program and to provide direction for the creation of materials and activities for the Young Astronaut Program. Although the Young Astronaut Program's aim is to stimulate interest in science, math, and technology, they consider their materials and programs to be a motivator in all subject areas. Chapters may be formed in schools or communities.

The Young Astronaut Council
P.O. Box 65432
Washington, DC 20036
(202) 682-1984 and Website at http://www.yac.org

Students For the Exploration and Development of Space (SEDS)
(High School and College Students)

SEDS is the world's largest space enthusiast organization for high school and college students and is governed entirely by students. SEDS primary aim is the education of students about the unique opportunities of space by providing educational materials, networking contacts, and a forum through which students can become directly involved in the international space community. SEDS activities include: the Space Topic Educational Program (STEP), an educational program, and the Space Program Series (SPS), providing materials to chapters on current topics. Individual chapters of SEDS may be formed for a low nominal fee and annual conferences are held. The organization publishes a newsletter, *SEDS NOVA*, covering organizational news and topical information on space technology. SEDS provides a Website featuring space imagery.

Students for the Exploration and Development of Space
77 Massachusetts Ave., W20-445
Cambridge, MA 02139
(617) 253-8897 or Website at http://seds.lpl.arizona.edu

National Space Society
(Open Membership)

The National Space Society is a space-advocacy organization that promotes the exploration and development of space. NSS is a consolidation of two prior groups, the National Space Institute and the L-5 Society. Their bimonthly publication, *Ad Astra*, provides an open forum for commentary on all phases of space activities.

National Space Society
922 Pennsylvania Ave., SE
Washington, DC 20003
(202) 543-1900 or Website at http://www.nss.org

7. Recommended Reading and Other References

The following books and periodicals represent a cross-section of readings on space and space-related topics.

General Reader

Allen, Joseph P., and Russell Martin. *Entering Space: An Astronaut's Odyssey.* New York: Stewart, Tabori and Chang, Publishers, 1984. Allen gives a running account of a Space Shuttle mission and includes a look at future missions and space equipment. Beautifully illustrated with space photographs and artist concepts.

Armstrong, Collins, and Aldrin, with Gene Farmer and Dora Jane Hamblin. *First on the Moon.* Boston: Little, Brown and Co., 1970. A personal account of preparation and completion of the first lunar landing.

Bean, Alan. *My Life as an Astronaut.* New York: Pocket Books, 1988. Bean's personal reflections on his astronaut career.

Bean, Alan, with Andrew Chaikin. *Apollo*. Shelton, CT: Greenwich Workshop Press, 1998. A collection of Al's art depicting the Apollo lunar missions.

Bova, Ben. *Welcome to Moonbase*. New York: Ballantine, 1987. Ben Bova does a super job in presenting a hypothetical instructional and orientation manual for workers arriving for their first duty tour at a future moonbase. Well-written, plausible, and technically accurate.

————. *First Contact: The Search for Extraterrestrial Intelligence*. New York: NAL, 1990. A collection of essays by leaders in the field dealing with our attempts to find intelligent extraterrestrial life.

Collins, Michael. *Liftoff: The Story of America's Adventure in Space*. New York: Grove Press, 1988. Collins gives an excellent summary of space exploration, including the contemporary background leading up to the first space ventures, and with projections well into the future. Human as well as technical aspects of spaceflight are covered.

————. *Mission to Mars*. New York: Grove Weidenfeld, 1990. Collins presents various approaches for a Mars mission and discusses the human and technological challenges of interplanetary flight.

————. *Carrying the Fire*. New York: Farrar, Straus, and Giroux, 1974. Collins, who orbited the moon while Neil Armstrong and Buzz Aldrin made the landing, gives his perspective of the first lunar-landing mission.

Cooper, Henry S. F. *Before Liftoff: the Making of a Space Shuttle Crew*. Baltimore: Johns Hopkins University Press, 1987. The preflight training and flight preparation activities for the Shuttle mission 41-G crew members are described.

Cortright, Edgar M. *Apollo Expeditions to the Moon*. Washington: NASA SP-350, 1975. Well-illustrated recap of technical issues and operational problems encountered during the Apollo program.

Duke, Charlie, and Dottie Duke. *The Moonwalker*. Nashville: Thomas Nelson Publishers, 1990. Duke (*Apollo 16* lunar module pilot) and his wife Dottie describe an astronaut family's experiences from highly personal perspective.

Hansen, Rosanna, and Robert Bell. *My First Book of Space*. New York: Simon & Schuster, 1985. Juvenile, (early school years). A broad elementary introduction to various space topics.

Irwin, James. *Destination Moon*. Portland, OR: Multnomah, 1989. Juvenile. Irwin describes his training and schooling to become an astronaut and his adventure in the *Apollo 15* voyage to the moon.

Joels, K. M., et al. *The Space Shuttle Operators Manual* (revised). New York: Ballantine, 1988. Well-illustrated manual about the Space Shuttle, technical features and operating procedures.

Kaplan, Judith. *Space Patches*. New York: Sterling Publishing, 1986. Presents illustrations and stories about the individual flight patches and other insignia.

Kelley, Kevin W., *Association Of Space Explorers. The Home Planet*. Menlo Park, CA: Addison-Wesley, 1988. Outstanding photographs of the Earth taken by astronauts and cosmonauts from many nations, accompanied by comments and observations from space travelers representing seventeen national groups.

Kerrod, Robin. *The Big Book of Space*. New York: Gallery Books, 1988. Juvenile (early school years): Well-illustrated elementary introduction to space and space travel.

Lebedev, Valintin. *Diary of a Cosmonaut: 211 Days in Space*. College Station, TX: PhytoResource Research, Inc., 1988. This book is the diary of Cosmonaut Lebedev, who flew on *Salyut 7* in 1982. The book describes personal feelings, technical problems, and operational difficulties as they occur and are resolved.

Lovell, James. *Lost Moon*. New York: Houghton-Mifflin, 1994. Lovell's personal account of the *Apollo 13* mission, which was made into the highly successful movie.

O'Neil, Gerard. *The High Frontier*. Garden City, NY: Anchor Books, 1982. This is the original book on space colonies. Today it doesn't sound as far-fetched as it did when this book was first published.

Oberg, James E., and Alcestis R. Oberg. *Pioneering Space*. New York: McGraw-Hill, 1986. Jim Oberg and "Cookie" Oberg cover a wide variety of human and technical issues; this is a very interesting and readable book with the topics ranging from human performance to robotics applications.

Oberg, James. *Red Star in Orbit*. New York: Random House, 1981. A readable and informative look at the Soviet space program, including discussions of several controversial topics related to Soviet objectives, motives, and conduct of space exploration and utilization.

————. *New Earths*. Harrisburg, PA: Stackpole Books, 1981. Oberg gives an excellent description of a futuristic approach to converting Mars and Venus into habitable planets for humans.

Pogue, Bill. *Astronaut Primer*. Tucson, AZ: Libration Press, L5 Society, 1985. Originally I wrote this to summarize the zero-g effects on crew members and their ability to perform work in space. It was used by engineers working on Space Station Freedom and the L-5 Society published it to raise funds.

Ride, Sally, with Susan Okie. *To Space and Back*. New York: William Morrow, 1986. America's first woman in space shares the experience of her Space Shuttle adventure.

————, and Tam O'Shaughnessy. *The Third Planet: Exploring the Earth from Space*. New York: Crown, 1994.

Schirra, Walter, with Richard N. Billings. *Schirra's Space*. Boston: Quinlan Press, 1988. Schirra takes a candid look at the U.S. space program and offers his own suggestions for establishing goals and priorities. Wally Schirra was the only one of the original seven astronauts to fly in Mercury, Gemini, and Apollo.

Schulke, Flip and Debra, and Penelope and Raymond McPhee. *Your Future in Space*. New York: Crown, 1986. Juvenile. A description of the U.S. Space Camp training program.

Shepard, Alan, and Deke Slayton. *Moon Shot*. Turner Publishing, 1994. Shepard and Slayton teamed up with Jay Barbree and Howard Benedict to write an account of events that surrounded the Apollo program.

Simpson, Theodore. *The Space Station*. New York: IEEE Press, 1985. A good treatment of the economic, political, social, and technological issues related to the development of a space station (Space Station *Freedom* focus) as an operating base for future as well as contemporary applications.

Stine, G. Harry. *The Space Enterprise*. New York: Ace, 1980. Stine covers a lot of ground in this brief volume, but he is the first writer to really focus on the economic factors and issues—for instance, financing space ventures. He presents a lot of novel approaches.

Reference

Belew, Leland F. *Skylab: Our First Space Station*. Washington: NASA SP-400, 1977.

Brooks, Courtney G., et al. *Chariots for Apollo: A History of Manned Lunar Spacecraft*. Washington, NASA SP-4205, 1979.

Cassutt, Michael. *Who's Who In Space: The International Space Station Edition*. New York: Macmillan Library Reference, 1999. A comprehensive compilation covering the international participants in space exploration.

Compton, W. David, and Charles D. Brown. *Living and Working in Space: A History of Skylab*. Washington, NASA SP-4208, 1985.

Connors, M. M., et al. *Living Aloft: Human Requirements for Extended Space Flight*. Washington, NASA SP-483, 1985.

Ezell, Edward C., and Linda N. Ezell. *The Partnership: A History of the Apollo-Soyuz Test Project*. Washington: NASA SP-4209, 1978.

Gatlin, Kenneth. *The Illustrated Encyclopedia of Space Technology (second edition): A Comprehensive History of Space Exploration*. New York: Orion Books, Crown Publishers, 1989.

Hacker, Barton C., et al. *On The Shoulders of Titans: A History of Project Gemini*. Washington: NASA SP-4303, 1976.

Hart, Douglas. *Encyclopedia of Soviet Spacecraft*. New York: Exeter Books, 1987.

Humphlett, Patricia E. *Astronauts and Cosmonauts Biographical and Statistical Data*. Washington: GPO, 1985.

Keithmaier, Larry. *The Aviation/Space Dictionary* (seventh edition). Blue Ridge Summit, PA: Tab Books, Inc., 1990.

Neal, Valerie, Cathleen Lewis, and Frank Winter. *Spaceflight: A Smithsonian Guide*. New York: Macmillan, 1995. An excellent sourcebook on unmanned and manned space flight. Well-illustrated with color photographs, illustrations, and drawings. Easy reading.

Sheldon, Charles S. *United States and Soviet Progress in Space: Summary Data Through 1979 and a Forward Look*. Washington: GPO, 1981.

———. *Soviet Space Programs*: 1976–1980. Washington: GPO, 1981.

———. *Soviet Space Programs*: 1966–1970. Washington: GPO, 1971.

———. *Soviet Space Programs*: 1971–1975. Washington: GPO, 1976.

———. *Soviet Space Programs*: 1976–1980. Washington: GPO, 1981.

Smith, Marcia. *Astronauts and Cosmonauts Biographical and Statistical Data*. Washington: GPO, 1981.

Still, Russell. *Relics of the Space Race*. Roswell, GA: PR Products, 1995. A reference book with all sorts of unusual data about people and space artifacts associated with the space program.

Swenson, Lloyd S., et al. *This New Ocean: A History of Project Mercury*. Washington: NASA SP-4201, NTIS, 1966.

Periodicals

Ad Astra ("To the Stars"), the magazine of the National Space Society (NSS). Bimonthly. National Space Society, 922 Pennsylvania Ave., SE, Washington, DC 20003 (202-543-1900). Special membership rates for students under twenty-two and seniors sixty-four and older.

Air & Space/Smithsonian. Bimonthly. Air & Space/Smithsonian, P.O. Box 53261, Boulder, CO 80322-3261.

Aviation Week & Space Technology. Weekly. *Aviation Week*, P.O. Box 503, Hightstown, NJ 08520-9899.

Final Frontier, the Magazine of Space Exploration. Bimonthly. *Final Frontier*, P.O. Box 534, Mt. Morris, IL, 61054-7852 (815-734-6309).

Space News. Weekly (tabloid format). Check rate before subscribing. The Time Journal Co., 6883 Commercial Dr., Springfield, VA 22159-0500 (703-750-8600).

Novels

Bova, Ben, and Bill Pogue. *The Trikon Deception.* New York: Tor, 1991. A thriller with setting focused onboard an internationally funded space station near the end of the twentieth century. The unique operational and technical factors imposed by microgravity (zero-gravity) are interwoven with the intrigue.

———. *Mars.* New York: Bantam, 1992. Realistic novel about the first human explorers to reach Mars.

Gibson, Edward G. *Reach.* New York: Doubleday, 1989. Gibson was the scientist pilot on the third *Skylab* mission and writes an absorbing novel with the knowledge and authority of someone who knows the topic. Plot is based on a mid-twenty-first century setting.

8. CATALOGS

For those who like to shop by mail the following catalogs or periodicals (with occasional catalog sections) are listed below. Model kits, books, patches, clothing, etc. are available. No endorsement is intended or should be implied.

National Space Society (NSS): The Space Shopping Catalog. Write or call: Aerospace Resources, International, 1514 Vivian Ct., Silver Springs, MD 20902. Phone orders: (301) 649-3796. Orders help support the National Space Society—excellent selection of items.

Air & Space/Smithsonian (see periodicals list). Write or call: Smithsonian Institution, Dept 0006, Washington, DC 20073-0006. Phone orders: (703) 455-1700.

U.S. Space and Rocket Center; U.S. Space Camp/Academy. Space Gear, the official catalog of the Space Camp, write or call: U.S. Space and Rocket Center, One Tranquility Base, Huntsville, AL 35807-7015. Toll-free phone orders: (800) 533-7281.

Final Frontier Space Materials (see periodicals list): the catalog of space exploration. Write or call: Final Frontier Space Materials, 2400 Foshay Tower, Minneapolis, MN 55402. Toll-free phone orders: (800) 24-LUNAR (245-8627).

Abbreviations

AFRSI—advanced flexible reusable surface insulation
BMMD—body mass measurement device
CRT—cathode ray tube
CRV—crew return vehicle
CST—central standard time
EMU—extravehicular mobility unit
ESA—European Space Agency
EVA—extravehicular activity
FCS—fecal containment system
GEO—geosynchronous Earth orbit
GMT—Greenwich mean time
GPS—global positioning system
HUT—hard upper torso
ISS—International Space Station (same as ISSA)
ISSA—International Space Station Alpha
JEM—Japanese Experiment Module
JSC—Johnson Space Center
LCG—liquid cooled garment
LCVG—liquid cooling and ventilation garment
MET—mission elapsed time
MFR—manipulator foot restraint
MMU—manned maneuvering unit
NASA—National Aeronautics and Space Administration
NASDA—Japanese space agency
PLSS—portable life-support system
RCS—reaction control system

RMS—remote manipulator system (robot arm)
SEDS—Students for the Exploration and Development of Space
SRMS—Shuttle remote manipulator system
SSRMS—Space Station remote manipulator system
RSI—reusable surface insulation
SAA—South Atlantic Anomaly
SAFER—simplified aid for EVA rescue
SETI—search for extraterrestrial intelligence
SRB—solid rocket booster
TAL—trash airlock
TPS—thermal protection system
UCD—urine collection device
UT—universal time
OMS—orbital maneuvering system

Index

11-99